You Can Take the Girl Out of the Mountains but You Cannot take the Mountains Out of the Girl

Growing Up in Appalachia East TN

Jennifer Kinsler

Copyright © 2017 Jennifer Kinsler

All rights reserved.

ISBN-10:1544764553
ISBN-13:978-1544764559

DEDICATION

This book is dedicated to the memory of my paternal Great-Grandmother, Ethel Johnson Owens, who was born and raised in the Appalachian Mountains of East TN in a hollow off the beaten path of Panther Creek Road. (Much of my time growing up was spent with her although my experiences vary from place to place and in interactions with other people in these mountains.)

CONTENTS

	Acknowledgments	I
1	The People of the Mountains	Pg 1
2	Panther Creek to Fox Branch	Pg 15
3	Down on the Farm	Pg 29
4	In the Mountains with Grandma	Pg 37
5	School Days	Pg 47
6	Memorable Moments	Pg 59
7	Appalachian Favorites	Pg 69
8	Hard Times in the Mountains	Pg 75
9	Mountain Girl	Pg 81
10	Family Photos	Pg 87

ACKNOWLEDGMENTS

First and foremost, I wish to thank my father, Randall Lucas, for never being too tired to tell me the stories of his past. He tackled each one with the most interesting enthusiasm and humor.

I've spent many hours visiting and speaking with various family members who transmitted our family history for future generations. I was blessed to be able to sit down with several elderly family members and listen to their stories before they passed on.

I wish to thank my sweet friend, Eva Heape, who moved here from Florida with her husband, Walt, in 2016 to volunteer with Of One Accord Ministry. She sacrificed her time and dedication editing my work, giving me insight, and helping me arrange the contents of my story.

1 THE PEOPLE OF THE MOUNTAINS

There's something about growing up in the mountains that cannot be compared with city living. The mountains hold peaceful moments but also present many challenges and difficulties. The views are certainly breathtaking, but mountain living isn't for everyone. One of the most breathtaking views I've ever seen happens to be on top of Goins Chapel near the city seat of Sneedville Tennessee. The cover photo for this book was taken at this location. In my opinion, it is one of the most beautiful views in Tennessee. This view in Hancock County reminds me of a musical scene in the movie "The Sound of Music" about the hills being alive with its sounds and scenery. Hancock County is undoubtedly an artist's paradise with its scenery and interesting places. Those of us who grew up living in the mountains are some of the most dedicated to the mountain ways of life. In fact, we hold dear to many of our customs, traditions, and deeply rooted religious values even if we move away into what some may term 'better suited grounds' where ways of living can be much simpler. If mountains could speak, especially my mountains (I'll refer to the area where I grew up as mine since they are so much a part of who I am), they would tell me that no matter how far away I go, they will always be with me and welcome me back home at any given moment.

The section of mountains I was born and raised in is referred to as the East Tennessee Appalachia Mountains (pronounced ap-uh-latch-uh by the mountain people). I grew up in a small town called Sneedville (Hancock County), which is known particularly for its Melungeon heritage. I never really understood the Melungeon term until much later in life. I do not believe myself to be an expert on the Melungeons. The word first appeared in print during the 19th century to describe people of mixed ancestry. Melungeons were considered by outsiders to be a mixture of European,

Native American, and African Ancestry. Back in the early pioneer days, the old folks didn't hear of the Melungeon term but referred to the white/dark mixed people as the "Pluto Family". My grandmother Ethel had never seen an African American person in their community during the early 1900s. She was out working in the fields as a young girl with the rest of the family and saw a black man for the very first time. It scared her so bad she ran to her mother Ida. There were not too many very dark skinned folks around at that time. There was one famous Melungeon on top of Newman's Ridge near the present day Vardy Historical Community named Mahalia Collins Mullins aka "Big Haley". She was known for her moonshine dealings and her 500lb+ size. It was rumored that she kept a moonshine faucet near her bed and sold the mountain drink from her bedroom window. Through the years, stories about Big Haley have caused more rumor than fact. In the documents of William P. Grohse, relatives confirm Haley as being a good woman who was trying to make an earnest living by selling 'shine'. Mahalia was married to John Mullins and they had about 20 children including one also named John, who was possibly one of the ones who brewed the shine for her to sell. She was also known for making apple brandy as the family had a large apple orchard on their property. The law came to arrest her several times to no avail due to not being able to get her out of her house. Authorities always stated she was "ketchable but not fetchable". When she died, part of the wall had to be taken down near the fireplace area to get her out of the house. Despite the rumors, she did have a proper burial on top of the ridge near her house. The house was later moved from the top of the ridge to the bottom and sits just across from the restored Vardy Church as part of their museum.

    Thinking of my own family line, my Grandma Ethel was born and raised within minutes of the Vardy area. Grandma Ethel's mother, my 2nd Great Grandmother, Ida, referred to the Melungeons as the muh-ladders (mulattos). She explained this as the result of one dark skinned person marrying a white skinned person and having mixed children. Some say the dark skinned part of the Melungeons were Indians while others say they were Moors or of African descent. Grandmother Ida's father was Benjamin Fletcher and his father was Henry Fletcher. The 1860 census lists Henry and his family living in Hancock and lists a neighbor, Brooks Delp (most likely spelled Delph today) as Mulatto. Grandmother Ida was, no doubt, familiar with the Mulatto term. Ida's 5th great grandfather on her mother's side was Paul Bunch, an early pioneer settler. Paul was my 8th great grandfather. One of our relatives currently owns a black cape that belonged to Paul Bunch's father John, who came from England and passed it down through the family line (see photo at the end of book). During a discussion I had with Pearl Martin, who grew up in the area near Newman's Ridge in the early 1900's and is also a relative of mine, she remembers "Melungeon

Ridge" off of Panther Creek Road, which is called Johnson Ridge today and may have been known as Newman's Ridge for a time. This ridge ran all the way from the Tennessee side of Newman's Ridge through the Vardy Community into Virginia on the Powell Mountain side. Pearl stated that Claude Collins was a Melungeon she grew up with and she often fixed (mended or straightened) clothes for him back in their school days. Claude Collins attended the Presbyterian Mission School in Vardy, graduated from the University of Tennessee, taught school in Hancock County and did a lot of Melungeon research and work with the Vardy Historical Community later in his life. He was also a founding member of the Hancock County outdoor drama "Walk Toward the Sunset". Claude received the first ever Lifetime Achievement Award from the Melungeon Heritage Association. I discovered I shared DNA with Claude (Mullins) Collins. Gedmatch confirmed Claude and I share chromosomes 16 & 18. Sadly, Claude passed away in 2017 before I had the chance to speak with him.

There is great controversy surrounding the "mysterious" Melungeon people of the mountains. This is due in part to them being looked down upon in early days just because of the color of their skin, which had much to do with specific laws during that time. Skin color has been scientifically proven to be only less than a .2% difference in physical characteristics (eye shape, facial features) as compared to different people groups all over the world. Melungeons aren't actually mysterious at all. Most Melungeons know where their ancestors came from or at least have some written/oral records that date back to a certain generation. Back in 1846, several Melungeon men were put on trial in nearby Hawkins County for illegal voting under the suspicion of being black or a free person of color. The case was dismissed after the hands and feet of those in question were examined to verify they were not African Americans. It seems our government as a whole may have created racism among various people groups by allowing specific laws to discriminate against them. During a bible study, I learned about some race issues. For example, in 1906, a young black man by the name of Ota Benga was put on display in a cage at a Bronx Zoo because of his appearance. Ota was part of a pygmy tribe and he could not speak English therefore he lashed out at the people to express his frustration of being locked up. A group of black clergymen led protests and threatened the zoo with legal action so he was let out of the cage but still he wandered around the zoo with the animals. He was eventually released. This poor soul grew up depressed so he committed suicide in 1916. In addition, the Scopes Trials back in the early 1920's enticed our own college campuses to teach African Americans as being a lower class of people and this may have led to a surge in racism and related laws later on. We are all one race, the human race. We are all one color, which is brown, but many shades of brown. We all came from the same God. Our creator made us unique with our own special

DNA. As people began to populate the earth they branched into different people groups developing their own set of customs and traditions- such as we see today. Environment can play a role in skin color depending on the region where individual people groups inhabited. Several local East Tennessee colleges have extensive studies relating to who the mountain Melungeons were and where they came from. Many scholars claim Melungeons came from Spain/Portugal. Some claim they are of the lost tribe of Israel. Others have created many stereotyped ideas about them. A few reporters have made up stories that give readers an interested but biased view about the Melungeons. During 1969-1975, an outdoor stage drama called "Walk Toward the Sunset" featured the story of the Melungeon people in the mountains. The goal of the play was to boost tourism and promote economic development in Hancock County. However, the drama closed due to lack of attendance, motels, restaurants, etc. within the county.

According to information listed with the Vardy Community Historical Society in Hancock County, there were 4 "tribes" of Melungeon families that started from Vardemon Collins. As the families grew, common last names were Collins, Gibson (Gipson), Goins, and Mullins. Other names under these tribes include: Anderson, Bales/Bell, Bunch, Delph, Denim, Hale, Harmon, Johnson, Moore, Mosley, Minor, Miser/Mizer, Nichols, Reed, Sexton, Trent, Weaver, and Williams. I have direct lineage to the Melungeon surnames Collins, Mullins, Bunch, and Johnson from both parents' sides. My 3rd great grandmother on my mother's side was Alabama Collins. She lived on Newman's Ridge closer to the Claiborne County side. Her father was Benjamin K. Collins, but not the same as Old Ben Collins who was one of the first early settlers of Newman's Ridge. My Ben may or may not have been related. However, Alabama's family was listed in the 1870 census as Mulatto's but were later listed as white. They may have changed the way their race was listed to keep from being harassed over who they were or because specific laws came into place that discriminated against them. Family oral tradition has stated Alabama to be a full blooded Cherokee Indian. The Cherokee were friendly Indians and Alabama's parents traveled with some early pioneers from the state of Oklahoma. Alabama's mother, Mary Jones, fled the Trail of Tears after her parents were shot in front of her. She stayed in a cave in Kentucky where part of her family also hid until they fled further into the Appalachia Mountains near Virginia and North Carolina (sections of Hawkins County was also North Carolina at one time) before settling on the Mulberry Gap Tennessee side of Newman's Ridge. I had my DNA tested in 2017. It showed I had a larger percentage of Western European descent with a mix of British (23%), Irish (14%), Scandinavian (6%), and African American (2%) background. I also had less than a 1% Spain/Portugal background. Further breakdown analysis revealed I have less than 1% Native American made up of three different tribes which are of the North American, Arctic, and South American Indians. This Native American breakdown may explain the 1% Spain/Portugal background that showed up as some tribes mingled with the Spanish and Portuguese soldiers in the 1500's. The Arctic comes from the 30 or more tribes of the 1600/1700's of which Pocahontas was a part. My genetic communities confirmed I was very likely a part of the Settlers of Northeast Tennessee and Southwest Virginia later as those states were established. I know that many of my early ancestors migrated from these areas and into Hancock County.

Some say the Melungeon people have a "third eye" which is a small bump or knot on the back of their head. The technical term is called an Anatolian Knot, which is a ridge on the base of the skull. I met one of our Tennessee State Senators during a 2016 Hawkins County Leadership class visit to Nashville Tennessee. During dinner one evening, he stated he had relatives from Hancock County and that he himself was a Melungeon because he had this "third eye" to prove it. He had me feel the back of his head. He briefly felt the back of my head as we sat at our dining table stating he could not find a knot on my head therefore, I must not be a Melungeon. I am unsure how to search for this knot nor had I ever heard of it. Some historians and researchers say the "third eye" is only a myth and hasn't been proven while others say all Melungeons have it.

In addition, Native American Indians had settled on this land in pre-Hancock County with the arrival of the pioneers. It is uncertain if there were Native Americans living here before the pioneers came. Daniel Boone's trail through the Appalachian wilderness along with his hunting party were the first ones to claim there were no other people in the area during early 1760. Sneedville Tennessee was once called "Greasy Rock" as there was a large rock in a creek where these hunters dressed their game. Many of the Indians came to the mountains so they could escape the government pushing for them to move out West. Suffering persecution much like the African Americans did, the Native Americans were considered to be savages or threats by some of the white men in government offices. Pioneer settlers who had dark skin were not allowed to vote, hold office, or testify in court against a white man. This is what forced some of the pioneers to move to the mountains as well. These settlers traveled by Indian Trails on foot through the Cumberland Gap. Some traveled by the Clinch-Powell-Holston Rivers to the Tennessee River at Knoxville then on to other areas in Middle Tennessee and Kentucky. The mountains was a place the Indians could safely hide. Some of the early pioneers simply inherited government granted land in exchange for their service in war. Much of the survival tactics used by the pioneer settlers were taught by the Indians. They were not only neighbors, but friends and companions. I remember going to school with Rain and Owl (Indian names), who are of the Kituwv/Shawano Indians. Although both were considered full-blooded, the Kituwv/Shawano were made of three different tribes, which included Cherokee. The brothers had to have American names because their Indian names could not be accepted. Unfortunately, they have had to relive the thoughts of their given Indian names being replaced with common American names in order for them to attend school. They preferred to go by their Indian names only but had no choice in the matter of school attendance. I only knew their American names during our school years together and later found out their Indian names. According to Rain, DNA doesn't seem to be accurate in identifying markers of indigenous American Peoples. There are things involved in genetic analysis that many indigenous cultures consider violations of their principles or values. Scientists found specific markers in human genes they call Native American markers because they believe all of the original Indians have these genetic traits. Many Natives intermarried with pioneer neighbors thus creating markers that would be mixed. Our traditions make us who we are, not our biology. Early census takers did not list Indian as a race on their paperwork but rather listed them as free persons of color or Mulatto. I had heard through oral tradition that my own family had Cherokee Indian blood on Grandmother Ida's side as well but it has yet to be confirmed. Many families from the Newman's Ridge area or Hancock County in general stake claim to having Cherokee Indian blood. Rain and Owl's father is a direct descendent of Cherokee war chief Dragging Canoe. During the Revolutionary War, Dragging Canoe fought on the side of the British and afterward raided white settlements along the Holston, Watauga, and Nolichucky rivers. Just recently (2017), the Amis Mill owner in neighboring Rogersville TN (Hawkins County) welcomed Rain and Crow's father and other locals with opening a monthly Big Creek Artisan Market on the grounds that will feature Cherokee crafts and other items. The Cherokee people were active traders at the Thomas Amis historical settlement in Hawkins County more than 200 years ago. Captain Amis was one of the few whites in the area that would trade with the Indians. The Amis Mill is a historical point of interest having the oldest stone dam in Tennessee with a one of a kind ebbing and flowing spring. It's also a great place to enjoy some good cooking and beautiful scenery!

    Hancock County was formed in 1844 from neighboring Hawkins and Claiborne Counties. Settlement actually began around 1795. Hancock County is made up of several smaller communities including Alanthus Hill, Kyles Ford, Mulberry Gap, and Treadway. Sneedville gets its name from W.H Sneed, an attorney from Knoxville who helped establish the county. The county was named for Revolutionary War patriot, John Hancock. Hancock County is considered to be a burned county, therefore there are few early records available. The Church of the Latter Day Saints can microfilm what few records had survived the fires in the early 1900s. The courthouse caught on fire at least two different times and flooded once. My great Grandmother Ethel's family lived near the Newman's Ridge area just off Panther Creek Road (Painter Creek as many mountain folk called it). Back in the early pioneer days there were many Black Panther sightings in the area, thus, its latter name. The entrance to Panther Creek is located about four miles east outside of the city seat of Sneedville. The Panther Creek area was also called Buffalo Creek during the Indians' time there. Grandma Ethel later lived in the community of Kyles Ford, along the Upper Clinch River, on Fox Branch Road until she passed away. This land was passed down to her and her siblings from the Fletcher's side. I spent the majority of my young life in the Kyles Ford area. Old tax records state Fox Branch as being "in the gap on Indian Ridge". There were Indian mounds on Panther Creek and Fox Branch so artifacts such as arrow heads were found to prove the Indians' existence there. One relative still has an old Indian Tomahawk that was passed down through the family from over 200 years ago.

Hancock County consists of six to seven thousand in population. Population hasn't increased or decreased that much over the years. It is one of the poorest counties, if not the poorest, in the state of Tennessee and ranks 27th poorest in the nation. The annual median household income is just over $14,000 and more than half of the residents continue to live in poverty today. At least 80-90% of the families receive some type of government assistance. Furthermore, geographic isolation created by the mountainous terrain along with few job opportunities and a lack of education make mountain living in this section of the mountains merely difficult but certainly not impossible. Despite these disadvantages, mountain life has made me very proud to be a mountain girl. I'm always excited to travel back home and, fortunately, I am not that far away. Many of my relatives still live in these mountains, including my parents.

My family (Dad, Mom, and I) lived in what we called "The green house", which was just next door to Grandma Ethel's (photos at the end of the book). This old house holds many memories dear to my heart, which I'll talk about more in later chapters. Grandma lived the latter part of her life in an antique (possibly 60-80's model) single wide mobile home she purchased from her nephew. Nestled beneath the mountains and just along Fox Branch Road, neither home had adequate plumbing. When stepping out of the back or front doors, the mountainous beauty could be seen all around. Walk out the front door about twenty to thirty steps and you will also be on the main public road that ran through the branch. Grandma owned close to one hundred acres that had been passed down to her or other relatives from her father, Singletary Johnson, who had inherited the 's, death. The Fox Branch land actually belonged to Ida ancestors. "Old" Jonathan Johnson (my 3rd great etary's father, owned nearly one hundred acres of the d in the 1880 tax records, which was most likely passed Indian Ridge ran all the way through Fox Branch and k. According to other relatives, Singletary and his brother Tom, at one ___ e, owned a majority of the land that ran up and down Panther Creek and nearly into Fox Branch on one side. This could have been passed down from the Johnson side of the family. Several Johnson men received land grants before the early 1800's and beyond. In fact, Johnsons were listed in records receiving land grants from the King of England for their service in the French and Indian war. Over the years, the land on Fox Branch and Panther Creek was sectioned off and handed down to family or sold to other families. Traveling up and down these roads is like stepping back into time when I was traveling with my Grandma Ethel to visit relatives or traveling to local areas. I realize this way of life is gone. Things are no longer the same in this little community. How I miss these mountain experiences. What I would give to have them back. They're priceless.

Most mountain people made their living by farming in the mountains. Tobacco was a major cash crop for many years and mountain folk raised cows, hogs, and chickens to feed their families. This was no different for my Grandmother Ethel. She had a house back in the holler (hollow is the proper pronunciation but keep in mind I still use mountain language!) and we often walked back there to pick gooseberries, get a drink from the spring, or just take a stroll. Some of the family lived in the old house in the holler for a short time when I was younger. I remember playing near or in the spring many times as I picked out and played with the periwinkles that were in it. I haven't seen gooseberry bushes since I ate from those particular ones. The fruit was much like a grape and just as tasty. The gooseberry bush has been listed as a federally threatened species for nearly three decades. It is so rare these days that it is only found growing naturally in Florida and South Carolina. My cousin Rob, which was grandma's grandson, raised tobacco back in this holler as well as in the holler that ran behind the green house. Later, tobacco was raised in the open field in front of the green house. I often rode on the back of the tractor helping set the tobacco plants into the soil. Sometimes, I'd be appointed to trail along behind the tractor making sure the setter placed the plants properly into the ground. Once the crop was grown, we had to sear/sucker it, later chop it down at the stalk, and spear it onto sticks to be hung in the barn and dried. After the tobacco was worked up, it would be hauled to the tobacco warehouse across the mountain in Rogersville Tennessee. Those families in living in Sneedville would often haul their tobacco to nearby Claiborne

County. It was closer for Rob to travel to Rogersville. I made several trips to Rogersville with Cousin Rob. We always had to unload the tobacco on the warehouse floor and get a slip of paper. We would wait our turn to have our tobacco checked by buyers to see how much money we would get from it. Many families had to use their tobacco money to pay off their debts. The drive to Rogersville would take at least thirty to forty minutes one way. It did not matter which way we traveled into Rogersville, we could not get there without crossing the mountain. The tobacco business began to decline on these small farms once the surgeon general came out with the warning against tobacco products in the 1960's. Very few small farms raise tobacco today.

Living in the isolated mountain area with few resources made it difficult for those who had to travel to get to areas with more resources; stores, or better jobs. Hancock County had more manufacturing jobs during the 1970-90 period. One local motor plant just outside the city seat of Sneedville (Morrell Motors) shut down and relocated to China. Many lost their jobs due to foreign trade. Hancock County also lies at the Virginia border, where Daniel Boone crossed into the American West and where coal mines existed farther south. Southern Virginia was known for its coal production where countless folks traveled for work until most of the coal mines closed down. As mountain folk would often say "it folded up". Numerous Hancock County residents' today drive outside the county to work in factories or hold other positions with higher pay while many of the elders receive social security income or disability and struggle to make ends meet. Gas stations are still very scarce in these mountains, meaning one has to fuel up at one local location before getting to their destination across the mountain. Those families living in the upper end of the county have to drive even farther to get gas. Growing up, I cannot remember a single gas station in operation other than Baker's Grocery. This store eventually closed and there are no fueling stations in the upper end of the county today. The closest one is just a mile or two outside the town of Sneedville when traveling to the Kyles Ford community.

Those who don't have a working knowledge about the mountains and its people have specific views about it. Some of those views are not very accurate while others are very biased. For example, some statistics and research show that 50-80% of mountain people are considered to be illiterate. Most mountain people could read the bible even if they couldn't read anything else. Their deeply held belief in God and his son, Jesus Christ, meant they needed to know what saith the word of God. The Bible of the mountain people must be none other than the King James Bible. This translation contains much of the Old English style language as spoken during that time period and for mountain folk to be able to read and understand it says much about them. The Stewart families living in

Hancock County in particular credit their own ancestor kinship to King James Stewart of Scotland. Don't ask the mountain folk to change versions or accept modern versions into their churches as the KJV has been around for more than four hundred years. Mountain folks believe it to be as close to the original translations in our English language. It is considered to be a word-for-word translation with the use of incorporating English words that meant the same or similar to the original words in the Hebrew, Aramaic, and Greek text. This is the only Bible the majority of us have ever known, read, or heard preached from during church services. If it's good enough for our ancestors to accept Christ and to live under, it is still good enough for us today. I continue to only use the KJV version as well. I do not take it lightly when someone laughs about it or refers to it as "The King's English" because I think it is beautifully written and the style of language should be taught to our children. I do understand translations are needed but also believe most publishing companies that produce the Bible in so many different versions are only doing it to make money. The English language has the most versions available today. Why do we need thousands of translations/versions in the English language alone? The Holy Bible is the number one selling book in the world. Most new versions (after 1900's) came from the KJV due to it not being copyright protected (public domain). With the creation of new words in our modern language the newer translations can quickly become too man-made, thus undermining the context and true meaning of the originals. Some things are better left alone, in my opinion. We have enough confusion. We have to be careful what we add or take away concerning God's word. I think most mountain folk would very well agree with me on this one. I often refer to the original Hebrew/Greek word meanings to deepen my understanding of the KJV text.

Some may think mountain people are dumb, uneducated, and close minded. I beg to differ. Mountain people are some of the most intelligent people I have ever known. We stand firm in what we believe. We are honest and hold true to our word. Mountain folk are very educated in mountain ways of living. They know how to grow their own food, make their own clothes, and make needed supplies during a time period when they could not rely on modern stores for what they needed. While many may not be well equipped in proper English or dialect, they came up with their own language, so to speak. Creating a language that outsiders sometimes wonder what is being said is in and of itself intelligent! I still use much of this language and it often humors outsiders while causing others to question what I said! I have found myself needing to explain my words more than once. I had a difficult time during my college years (age 28-35) with the proper enunciation and with "–ing" endings in particular. I often leave off the "-ing" as it seems easier to say workin', playin', listenin', etc. I had one teacher in college, Mrs. Brown aka "The Grammar Police" who wrote me up every single time during my student teaching observations for leaving off the "-ing", although I received straight A's from her! This was, after all, my home language so why would I need to change the way I talk to suit higher education standards? Of course, I needed to know it in order to teach it to school children and so I learned as much as I could about it. The school children where I grew up also spoke the same way I did and continue to do so today. I've even heard of some folks who grew up in these mountains but later moved away who tried real hard to cover up their southern drawl to the point they began talking with a more proper accent and always had correct grammar usage. We should never be ashamed of who we are and where we came from nor how we speak. I graduated with a near perfect GPA in my undergraduate work. I went on to receive my Masters in Education not long after obtaining my Bachelor's in Education. I taught in an elementary school while I was working on my master's and raising two children. I have credits from a total of three colleges. If I can get through college, anyone can. Most of us aren't toothless nor do we wear overall's and stand on the side of the road barefooted while picking a banjo. This is a mountain stereotype created by outsiders. In fact, many outsiders have been known to make fun of the people in the mountains of Tennessee. There was an incident at one of the schools in Hawkins County involving children being served outdated cafeteria pork. It was an oversight on the part of cafeteria management and quickly addressed while no one became ill from eating it. Cafeteria staff even ate some of it themselves. However, as the news went national, one comedy channel picked up on it and made fun of how one of our area County Commissioners (who actually attended school in Hancock County) spoke. This comedy station used vulgar language throughout their joking while making the statement "I don't speak Tennessee" "Can anyone translate?" followed by a picture of a cartoonish banjo playing by itself and thanking the "translator banjo" for interpreting the language. Near the end of the comedy clip, the guy said "If you've ever eaten at a public school in Eastern Tennessee please seek medical attention immediately. This is not a joke. You could be sick and/or dying." For some children in the mountains, the food they ate at school may have very well been the only meal they were able to eat that day. Our local ministry in Hawkins County that also serves Hancock County (Of One Accord Ministry) provides a summer feeding program for Hawkins County children once school is out to make sure they are fed until school starts again in the fall. It is a goal of the ministry to have the program in Hancock County eventually as funding and resources become available.

 A friend of my daughter's moved to California recently. She was working through a rental car agency. A lady came in from Burbank California- which is a wealthy neighborhood. A brand new SUV rental was awaiting the lady, but she noticed it had a Tennessee license plate. She walked around the vehicle and decided she did not want it because she thought it was "ugly". When my daughter's friend questioned her about it the lady stated she could not drive it because "it has TN plates on it" and she can't be driving around California with TN tags as people would think she was a "hillbilly redneck". My daughter's friend simply told the lady that she was from Tennessee in the heaviest southern accent she could use (on purpose). After she showed her some other rental options the lady decided she would just take the rental with the TN tags. In turn, she asked the lady if she was sure as she might be sayin' "ya'll" by the time she returned! The lady quickly apologized by stating how rude she had been and left with the TN plated rental. Although generations of mountain folks have been ridiculed for their dialect, just a couple of years ago, Walt Wolfram with the North Carolina State University referred to Appalachian mountain language as "highly systematic grammar that is quite patterned." Linguists now state there's really no wrong way to talk. We are all unique and very diverse in our languages.

My Grandma Ethel survived and lived in the mountains until she was eighty-three years old. She did not take into consideration how she talked, or cussed, for that matter. As far as I know, she never went to college or trade school but she hoped her children and grandchildren would. Mountain people are just like anyone else in that they too have specific dreams for their offspring. Grandma had dreams for her son Harold to become a medical doctor and for her daughter Betty to become a nurse. Although this didn't happen, several in our family went to college and received degrees. I was the very first one in our family to receive a college degree. Later, Aunt Diana (Betty's daughter) went to college and received her RN degree while Cousin Stacy (Harold's daughter) received her degree in Physical Therapy. My oldest daughter, Ashley, now has her RN degree and is a traveling nurse in a program through a local college that serves eight counties working with first time mothers. She has recently gone back to school to work on her Master's in Nursing. My youngest daughter, Rebecca, just finished her first year of college and she is majoring in Psychology with a minor in Sociology. She made the Dean's List. One of my favorite classes from my college years was Sociology because we were able to learn about our surrounding community functions. Rebecca is a gifted artist as well as an independent singer/songwriter. She can draw or paint anything she looks at or visualizes and she has an amazingly beautiful and unique voice. Grandma's dream wasn't in vain but happened in a much different way than she would have ever known. I have no doubt she would be very proud of us today. I expect to see more of her grandchildren obtain some type of degree and maybe one day one of them will actually become a medical doctor.

Many before and after Grandma Ethel's time have survived living their entire lives in the mountains as well. Mountains are much like the arms of a loving mother or grandmother. They wrap around you and hold you in place and give you a sense of security. This is what my mountains did for me. I didn't mind if I had never left the mountains. The memories of my mountains are etched in a corner of my soul along with all those who made each memory so much sweeter.

You Can Take the Girl Out of the Mountains But You Cannot take the Mountains Out of the Girl

2 PANTHER CREEK TO FOX BRANCH

Mattie Ethel Johnson was born to Singletary and Ida (Fletcher) Johnson on July 26, 1913 in Blackwater Virginia (A section of Hancock County also had a Virginia address for many years). Singletary and Ida were born and raised in Hancock County (originally Hawkins County during some of these years) during the late 1800's. Ethel was the 5th of 14 children. Four of these children (3 boys and 1 girl) died either at birth or early childhood. Back in those days, Typhoid Fever, Measles, and Tuberculosis were common illnesses that often led to death. Mountain people either had lack of medical help where they lived or it took too long for a doctor to reach them or for them to get to a doctor. People with illnesses often died before receiving help. Because of this, mountain people relied on home remedies that may or may not have helped depending on the illnesses. Ida developed appendicitis so she had to travel across the mountain to Rogersville to have surgery. She was four and a half months pregnant with one of her sons, Roy, when she had the surgery. Roy was named after Dr. Roy Doty in Rogersville because she felt that the Doctor saved her life. She stated she was ready to go (prepared to meet the Lord) as their family was Christian and attended the Baptist church. Roy lived to be about three years of age before he died. He had some type of problem with his throat. Singletary always said the cat had taken the baby's breath so he hated cats from that point on. This was an old wives fable. Back then, many people accepted old wives tales as fact.

Old Jonathan was a cabinet maker in the 1860's. Jonathan's father was originally from North Carolina but I have no record of him or his name. It was stated that Jonathan's father may have gone to Texas. Jonathan may have had a brother named James but we are uncertain. "Old Jonathan" had two families going at the same time. Jonathan was married to

Jane "Jenny" Bloomer but also had children by Elizabeth "Betsy" Pratt, who lived next door to them. He was called "old" as he was said to have lived to be well into his 90's. Fathering illegitimate children was unheard of during those days as mountain people never spoke about such things. The church did not accept such acts from Christians and dealt with them according to biblical principles. The member would be expelled from the fellowship of the local church if he/she refused to repent of his/her deeds after consulted. Old Jonathan kept his deeds a secret for many years. However, his first wife, Jane, found out about it and it was told that when she got mad at Jonathan she would tell him to "just go on up the hill to Elizabeth". (If our churches of today would continue to deal with such matters as in old days, we would see less of it and more of God's blessings on our lives). I have no record of Jonathan Johnson beyond the 1880 census. Jane filed for divorce in 1882 and not long after this Old Jonathan married Betsy Pratt, according to family as well as research documents put together by Taylor/Grohse that are on record in Hancock County Tennessee. Oral tradition passed down through our family states Jonathan and Betsy married when their youngest son, John, was about four years old. Jonathan and Besty had twelve children by the time they married. Betsy had a son named Singletary, who was my great great grandfather. Betsy's children and grandchildren were often made fun of by locals most likely due to what their father had done. Aunt Jeanette Johnson (Singletary's daughter) recalled as she was coming home from school one day, she stopped to pick a pear from a tree. Other children were picking pears as well and began to make fun of her by calling her Jeanette Pratt. This hurt Jeanette's feelings as well as made her mad. She told me she finally forgave them as that is what Christians must do. Although Jonathan's children took the Johnson name once he and Betsy wed, they were referred to as "Pratt's" for many years after. Census records show the children going from Pratt to Johnson. The Pratt women were known to keep their maiden name, even after marrying. The Pratt's lived up on Melungeon ridge and Polly Pratt (Betsy's mother) was a midwife in the community. Polly would often stay with expectant mothers through the birthing process and some days beyond if needed. Grandmother Ethel certainly did not like being referred to as Ethel Pratt either. She was born a Johnson legitimately. She would cuss you out in a second if she heard you call her Ethel Pratt!

One of Old Jonathan's sons by Betsy Pratt was Singletary. Singletary and Ida reared their children in a one room sawmill lumber home built around 1870-1880 (see photo). The home was built by Singletary's father, Jonathan Johnson, when Singletary was around two years of age. Less than a quarter of a mile from Singletary & Ida's home was a working sawmill at Stewart Farm. Pioneer Boyd Stewart was known for his coopering trade of making baskets, chairs, and other items that helped furnish a lot of these area homes. Boyd's grandson, Alex Stewart, later learned the coopering trade that helped many of the families that lived through the upper 1900's. Alex used his own hand tools to make anything from furniture to weapons to toys out of wood. If someone died, Alex would build a coffin for the family. Alex's wife, Margie, was my Grandpa Singletary's niece. Singletary and Ida's home was located just off Panther Creek Road not far north of the Vardy Community on Newman's Ridge. Singletary's brother, Tom, and his family lived on the flat of the ridge past Singletary and Ida's home. Most of the old mountain folks referred to this cabin as the "Tom Pratt Cabin" and many still do today. Tom's cabin is no longer there. Walking the ridge back in those days would have been a good hike but familiar grounds to many pioneers as they used its land for their resources and visited their neighbors.

Singletary & Ida's home mid-late 1900's.

Singletary & Ida's old home in 2013

Singletary was a farmer and Ida kept up the house and fed their large family. They raised a 6-8 acre garden and grew many rows of Irish potatoes. In addition to the family helping, Ida often hired Tom's son, Odas, to help dig the potatoes. She paid him $1 per day. Odas was said to be a very good worker. Ida grew sweet potatoes that were so big they had to be cut with an axe. Just one sweet potato would make a "mess" for the whole family of sixteen. They raised hogs and fed them slop (leftover table scraps), weeds, and corn. The hogs had to reach up to four hundred pounds in weight before they could be killed. They often shared their "hams of meat" with other families in the community. They owned an old milk cow Singletary had received from a trade. During hot summer days, the family would go out back to the wash house to cook and eat their meals so the main house would remain cool for sleeping at night. Folks in those days enjoyed natural air conditioning! They did not have the luxury of air conditioning many modern homes have today. They often had spring houses, which were wooden planks built over the spring where they kept the cow milk cold by placing a container of it into the cold mountain water. Singletary's property had the best spring on Panther Creek. Neighbors tapped into it so they could have good water as well. During those days, neighbors came together and helped one another out in times of need. Often they repaid each other by helping out with farming or by exchanging what resources they had available such as food or supplies.

Ida owned two sewing machines and made clothes for the children. She made shorts for the boys but Uncle Homer (grandma's brother) told me he hated them! She made dresses for the girls. Ida taught the girls how to sew. Later in their lives, some of the girls/boys went to work in a weave shop in South Carolina. Uncle Homer told me he had also worked in the weave shop filling batteries for a short time. To fill a battery, one had to wind the thread around several pointed bobbins that were in machines and keep them going at a fast rate of speed. There were at least sixty-nine sets of bobbins going at one time that needed threading.

The family attended regular meetings at Panther (Painter) Creek Missionary Baptist Church in Kyles Ford. When revivals were held in those days, five to six preachers would often be on the floor preaching at the same time. This mountain preaching would last for two hours or more. According to Uncle Homer, the preachers would really preach with the spirit and many people accepted the Lord as a result. People not only knew and taught the Bible but they also lived it. Even those who did not live it highly respected those who did. Back then, people had a genuine fear of God and wanted to please him above all else. God was all they had in the mountains besides family, friends, and food to survive. Singletary and Ida later attended church at Fox Branch Baptist where they were members when they died. Fox Branch recently received a plaque for 125 years of establishment. The church still has an outdoor toilet (outhouse).

When the children were school age, they had to walk a mile and a half to get to school. There were only two or three families who actually owned a car back then. Uncle Homer recalls George Mathis and Sam Stewart being the only ones who owned a car on Panther Creek. He could even remember seeing the car come down the road for the very first time and he thought that was something! The school the children attended was located on Dry Branch just off Panther Creek Road. Most places of worship back in those days also served as the school building during the week. Panther Creek Baptist Church had its own school building behind the church. It was later torn down. Teachers did not have a formal education degree but could volunteer to teach the children in the very early days while some went to receive an education later on. Some of those who taught school during the mid-1900s were Evelyn Baker, Hubert Greene, and Elmer Jaynes. Uncle Homer remembers one of his teachers, Elmer Jaynes, very well. The school day lasted from 7 or 8 am until 4 pm each school day. They broke for lunch for one hour and had two thirty minute recesses (evening and morning). Uncle Homer remembers the teachers were paid $5.25 per day! He was privileged to be in a play during his school days. His teacher, Mr. Jaynes, considered him to be very intelligent. The play was called "A Fortunate Calamity" and was twenty-six pages long. Uncle Homer remembered his lines well. His memory at the age of eighty-nine was just as clear when I visited with him to listen to his stories. In the school play, Uncle Homer played the part of a colored (negro) boy and Pearl Johnson (later married to John Martin, whose grandfather John once ran Martin's store at the forks of Panther Creek Road) played the part of a colored girl.

Pearl's brother-in-law was a legendary bluegrass singer and native of Hancock County, Jimmy Martin. There's a sign that stands at the entrance of Sneedville coming in from Highway 31 that reads "Hancock County Home of Jimmy Martin, King of Bluegrass & Home of the Melungeons". Pearl's father, Fate Johnson, was also a grandson of Old Jonathan Johnson by his first wife, Jane Bloomer. According to Pearl, Fate's stepmother's children bore the last name of Pratt and they often "kidded one another" about it. Brothers Vol and Frank Stewart were also some of Uncle Homer's classmates as well as relatives. Uncle Homer talked about what a smart man Frank always was. Frank brought some of his family to our Johnson Reunion back in 2013. He sat beside me listening intently the whole time as I showed a PowerPoint slide of our family photos. He would tell me stories about some of the people or say he remembered them well.

Singletary's brother, Nathaniel, loved the children so he often helped watch over them. Nathaniel was kicked in the head by a cow when he was younger and his mind was never the same after this accident. He never married and always stayed with some of the family until his death.

Nathaniel did not like for any of the children to get a whipping so he often told Singletary or Tom (Singletary's brother) they better not whip them. Nathaniel would often help with Tom's three children. One day Tom's son, Dewey, got a spanking from his teacher at school. Dewey told Tom about it the next morning so Tom made a trip to the school. The teacher asked him if he had "come to talk to him about Dewey" so Tom replied, "No, I've come to kill you. You're not going to be spanking my little Dewey anymore!" The teacher jumped out the window and little Dewey never got any more spankings once the teacher came back to school to teach.

Grandma Ida developed diabetes and died in her 60's. Her niece, Nora was spending the night and had slept in the bed with her. Ida was supposed to wake Nora up for school but she had become unconscious in her sleep. Grandma Ida died later that day. Nora woke herself up the next morning and explained to her father Edgar that "Grandma didn't wake up and take her medicine". The funeral was held at Singletary & Ida's home on December 05, 1947. It was customary in the early days to hold the body at the home of the deceased. The funeral service industry was relatively new. The Reverend James Ferguson officiated and Colboch Price Funeral Home in Rogersville TN was in charge. Ida was buried in the family cemetery (Johnson Graveyard as it was referred to). I have a copy of the memorial booklet and found a lot of the neighbors listed as visiting or making calls to the home to pay their respects. The newer generation of today doesn't seem to pay their respects like the older ones did. Back in those days if someone died the whole neighborhood took time off work/chores to go visit and the women prepared food to take to the family so they would not have to worry with cooking for a few days. The address at the time of Ida's funeral was listed as Blackwater, Virginia, but is now Kyles Ford Tennessee. Singletary remarried later on and died of old age. He was buried next to Ida in the family cemetery. Nine of the surviving children each married and raised their own families. Woodrow was never married.

You Can Take the Girl Out of the Mountains But You Cannot take the Mountains Out of the Girl

Children of Singletary & Ida:

Birdie Johnson (1906-1946) married Homer Anderson

Edgar Johnson (1908-1986) married Arkie Gibson

Katherine Johnson (1909-1994) married Elmer Stewart

Amanda Johnson (1911-2000) married Ralph Gibson Sr

Mattie Ethel Johnson (1913-1996) married Marvin Owens

Roy "Doty" Johnson (1915-1917)

Woodrow Johnson (1917-1988) never married

Fannie Pearl Johnson (1918-2005) married Willard Baker

Emory Johnson (1920-1920)

Julia Johnson (1921-2016) married John Parham

Lee Ray Johnson (1923-1923)

Homer Johnson (1924- 2015) married 1. Imogene Lawrence 2. Hazel Kinsler Larkey

Jeanette Johnson (1926-2015) married Herbert Eaton

Gracie Johnson (1928-1928)

Family Photo

Grandma Ethel and her sister, Julie, went to South Carolina to work in the cotton mill sometime during the 1920-1930s. The cotton mill may have been called Startex Mills, formerly Tacapau Mills, since Julie retired from there. This mill opened in the late 1800's and closed in 1998 due to foreign imports. The word Tucapau meant "strong" in Native American Language. Startex Mills was known for making cloth tea towels. Grandma first worked at Borden Mills in Kingsport Tennessee before she transferred to Spartanburg South Carolina. The sisters were battery fillers in the South Carolina mill. While initially there, Grandma and Julie lived in a boarding house. This cotton mill is where Grandma Ethel most likely met Grandpa Marvin Owens. She was only sixteen years old when she married Marvin, who was twenty-five, or younger as I think he may have changed his date of birth in order to work in the cotton mill. Marvin had worked in the cotton mill since the early 1900's and Spartanburg South Carolina was his original home place. Marvin was a cloth folder, a second hand, and later worked in the office at the mill. Marvin and Ethel lived with Dargan (Marvin's brother) and his family until they found their own place. They rented a home during the late 1930-1940's. They had two children together. Harold and Betty were born in Spartanburg, South Carolina. Marvin and Ethel lived in Spartanburg, South Carolina, during the presidency of Franklin D. Roosevelt when the United States declared war on Japan just one day after the attack on Pearl Harbor that killed 2,400 Americans.

Cotton was King in the South and working in South Carolina most likely paid higher wages than what was paid in any Tennessee industries. While working for a higher wage, one had to sacrifice their health to do so. Brown Lung was a common result of breathing in the air full of cotton dust that resulted in wheezing, coughing, and sometimes death. In the early days of working in the textile mill, employees were paid with tokens that could only be used at the company store. Grandma Ethel was listed in the early census as "non-employed for pay" so she may have worked for the tokens to get things she needed or wanted. In 1940, she earned $208 per month while Marvin earned $650. Employees worked twelve hour shifts six days per week. Many women dominated the textile industry beginning in the 1920's. My 2nd great grandmother, Ida, also went to work for a short time in the mill. Her daughter, Jeanette, was born in Cowpens South Carolina during their stay there in 1926.

Julie also met her feller (husband John) there and she remained in South Carolina to raise her family and lived there until her death. She was the last child of Singletary and Ida's to pass away. Most of the children lived to be close to eighty years of age or beyond with the exception of Birdie. Birdie had a preexisting illness (Typhoid Fever) and was later stung by a hornet, which made her health condition worse. Her daughter Irene recalls as her mother Birdie was working in the kitchen she saw the hornet come in and sting her on the forehead. Birdie stayed in bed for weeks after this. She died at the age of forty, leaving behind a husband and two children, Irene and Curtis. Grandma Ethel often made it a point to make sure Irene and Curtis were being well taken care of. Irene would often go stay with grandma in Church Hill. Irene says Grandma Ethel was one of her favorite aunts. She added that grandma made her dresses, skirts, and blouses to wear. Grandma would take Irene to the movies or out to eat once she got off work for the day. Irene never received a whipping from Grandma Ethel as she always tried to behave so grandma would never get mad at her. Jeanette's daughter, Sheila, also said Grandma Ethel was her favorite aunt. If she got into trouble with her own mother, she knew she could go to Aunt Ethel to help her out! Grandma had a way of spoiling the children.

At some point, Grandma Ethel moved back to Tennessee with the two children. They lived on Panther Creek for a brief time in a cabin on the old Anderson farm while Marvin was away in the army. They soon purchased some property in Church Hill, Tennessee. Grandma Ethel had a brick house built and later a smaller house was built behind it. When soldiers were shipped off, women were left to manage the home front. Grandma's Brother, Homer, helped with the mortar (laying brick) at the red brick house. Grandma lived there with their two children, Betty and Harold. Soon after Grandpa Marvin passed away, Grandma Ethel moved back to Fox Branch in Kyles Ford Tennessee. Betty later married Paul Lucas and they had three children: Randall, Diana, and Marvin Eugene (Goob). Randall is my dad. Betty and Paul moved into the smaller house behind the red brick house in Church Hill for a while before moving back to the green house in Kyles Ford. Harold had four children: Robert and Patricia by Gale Gonce and later had Stacy and Angie by his second wife, Illene Tankersley. Harold was given the red brick house in Church Hill, Tennessee, where he raised his family but he later moved back to Kyles Ford to live near Grandma Ethel after the children were grown.

The green house was built on the family farm on Fox Branch between the 1950-1960s. This was an old board and bat house. The boards appeared to be a light green color, which is where it got its name. Betty and Paul lived in the green house until Betty's death. There were other houses built in the holler on Fox Branch where other relatives lived for a short time. Grandma lived in one of the houses herself for a short while before moving into her mobile home. Grandma Ethel was known to help her family by allowing them to live in these homes as long as they needed to. During 1933, a cyclone (possibly a tornado type) came through and destroyed some of the homes on the branch and surrounding areas. Grandma Ethel was in South Carolina when this happened. Harriet Fletcher's sister, Rachel Pridemore,

Grandma Ethel's aunt, died from injuries she received during this cyclone while she lived in Harriet's house at the mouth of the holler. Uncle Homer remembers helping build the house back when he was just a young boy. Two soldiers were shot and killed at this old house during the Civil War. They were hooking up their wagon when someone came by and shot them. No one knows where they were buried. Old Ben Fletcher, Harriet's husband, ran the family moonshine still on some of the Fox Branch property that he inherited from his father, Henry. I have yet to find out if Grandma Ethel's land was the same land where Henry Fletcher was buried. When Ben was 80 years old he was raided by Sheriff Fate Johnson as he was slopping the hogs. Old Ben could not run due to his age so he was taken to jail where he was held until released on bond. Ben pleaded with the law to keep his still and worm as it was his father's inheritance to him. The still and worm (a coiled copper tube that distills the moonshine) was confiscated by the law. Ben came home, got sick and died just before the trial. Harriet was able to keep the land and it was passed to her daughter Ida at her death and on down to my Grandmother Ethel and her siblings. Harriet is buried just up the road near the Delph and Moles family homes. Some of the Fletchers or possibly Fishers were buried across the road from grandma's trailer on Fox Branch but the graves are unmarked. It was said that a house fire was the result of two women's deaths. These women are buried here in addition to two other unknown people.

Grandpa Marvin Owens passed away of a heart attack in his sleep just before being able to retire and come back home from service. This happened in Fort Hood Texas in 1965, leaving Grandma Ethel to continue raising grandchildren on her own. Grandpa Marvin was brought home to Church Hill on a train accompanied by two sergeants. The two men stayed with the family the entire time and had even brought toys for all the children. His funeral was held in Hancock County and he is buried in the Johnson Cemetery off Panther Creek Road. Grandma decided to move back to Fox Branch soon after Marvin's death. She received an army pension along with insurance that allowed her to do this. She also received settlement money from Marvin's death. She originally contemplated purchasing a restaurant where the old laundry mat in Sneedville, Tennessee, is now. Betty and Paul had already moved back to live in the green house before Grandma Ethel moved back. Grandma did not want her daughter Betty driving across the mountain and back six days per week to work. However, they changed their mind and she purchased Betty a 1958 Pontiac instead of the restaurant. They must have felt it would be too complicated to run a business. Grandma Ethel purchased additional shares of land that connected to her Fox Branch property that some of her siblings were willing to sell. She bought a few extra acres from Bedford Livesay who had owned property back in the holler behind the old house where Piney

Johnson lived. Piney was grandma's niece. Bedford was an old man and lived by himself back in the ridge. No one had been to check on him in a while so once someone did, they found him dead of old age. A rat had nearly eaten his entire ear off when they found him. With losing her husband and with a family to raise and feed, grandma decided to remain living on Fox Branch with the resources she had available. She never remarried after this. She outlived both her children. She lived in the mountains as a strong, independent, pioneer woman with a great determination to survive, and so she did.

Ethel Johnson Owens

Betty Lucille Owens

Marvin and Ethel Owens

Randall, Eugene, and Diana

Top Left to Right: Paul and Betty Lucas at the green house, Trish (my mom), Aunt Diana, Mammaw Betty
Middle L to R: Randall & Trish (Dad & Mom), Jennifer (me)
Bottom L to R: Randall Paul Lucas, Jr; Jessica Lucille Lucas inside green house (my siblings)

You Can Take the Girl Out of the Mountains But You Cannot take the Mountains Out of the Girl

Jennifer Kinsler

3 DOWN ON THE FARM

Being a single woman trying to raise a family in isolated mountains was not easy. Grandma Ethel had to help raise her grandchildren while her daughter and son worked. Five adventurous children with enough curiosity to kill a cat was rather emotionally draining, to say the least. It was no wonder grandma sometimes cussed (cursed with words). Her favorite word was "hell" when she got real mad! She was one of the kindest and most generous people on the branch but don't dare make her mad or you were sure to know about it. Many people spoke very well of her and remember how good she was to everyone. She did not use the switch or belt sparingly when disciplining the children. She didn't mind raising her voice to get their attention, either. It did not matter that the whole neighborhood up and down the branch may have heard her "hollering". One day, the children decided they would sneak off to the creek near Baker's Grocery but grandma caught up with a couple of them. Aunt Diana and Cousin Trish were the ones to get their legs "switched good". The boys got away before she caught them. Often, when grandma was ready to go somewhere the children could hear her start her old red station wagon. She would get in, put the foot pedal all the way to the floor, turn the starter, and rev up the motor so loud the children thought sure it was going to blow up!

One time, she was in bed trying to rest after not feeling well and had left the children in one of the nearby rooms to play on their own. My Dad was the oldest and probably about 12-13 years old at the time. Dad and Rob decided they would put axles and wheels on grandma's recliner. They used the red reflectors off their bicycles to add to it as well. Trish and Diana helped push/ride the recliner through the house after it was made into a car. They pushed their new "car" just as fast as it would go while bumping into the walls every now and then. The ceilings in the house were about seven foot from the floor, meaning they were hung low. Grandma kept hollering and telling the kids to quit but they didn't seem to want to listen too well. Needless to say, she got up, went outside and came back in with an axe and gave the recliner a few licks (hits) while also ramming the axe into the ceiling tearing some of the drywall and light socket out. She then pushed the recliner on out the back door. Her exact words: "G-damn it, I told you all to quit!" I'd say the kids never tried to make another car out of a recliner again! Needless to say, it would not be long before the children figured out something else to do with their time that was equally as aggravating to grandma.

Another time, the children were playing in the bathroom. It was thundering outside so Grandma Ethel blamed the kids for making all the noise. She told them they better quit making all that racket (noise). The children tried to tell her it wasn't them. All of a sudden a big crack of thunder boomed and grandma yelled at the kids and grabbed some plates and cups and threw them all over the house!

On one other occasion, some of the children had managed to get inside of one of Grandma's old junk cars. She had quite the collection of old cars sitting around everywhere. I assumed when these cars quit running that is where they remained and parts were sold from them. Robert was sitting on the trunk lid to hold it down with the girls inside. He and my dad lit a handful of dry grass and held it up to one of the missing tail lights. Thankfully, the car had been stripped of parts including the gas tank! The girls told that the boys were trying to set them on fire. This wasn't what the boys intended as they were just playin' around to teach the girls a lesson about hiding inside a trunk! I think it just scared the girls real bad so they were finally let out!

While the children were often adventurous, Grandma tried to keep them busy doing things that would teach them responsibility and hold their interest. She raised hogs and cattle so she decided to purchase a young sow pig for each of the children to help take care of. This was exciting for the children. Dad (Randall) remembers his pig was black with a white stripe. Robert and Diana's were both black. Goob had a solid white pig. Once the sows had their babies they would sell for $12.50 per pig. My dad remembers his sow having nine to eleven pigs at a time. The children could then take their money to Cash–N-Tote in Sneedville to buy school clothes they needed. Many families purchased clothing, shoes, and household items from this store. The most popular Cash-N-Tote children's item from my day were the purple Kangaroo shoes that had a "secret pocket" in the tongue of the shoe with a zipper. This was a place we could keep our quarters safely without losing them. Cash-N-Tote went out of business around 2008 and is now The Shepherds Corner thrift store operated through Of One Accord Ministry with headquarters in Rogersville TN. I am currently employed through this ministry. We serve two counties (Hawkins and Hancock) with a variety of programs that help those less fortunate.

A favorite trip for the children was going to the bread store in nearby Blackwater, Virginia. The store sold candy so grandma would buy the children some of it. Normally, on the way back home, grandma would stop at the old sewing factory in Virginia (Pins and Needles) to get free quilt pieces. This was also an old school building at one time. The sewing factory shut down between 1993-1995. The factory often had scraps left over after employees cut out the patterns they needed. They would give grandma clear 4-5 foot long bags of fabric scraps that she would use to sew together to make quilts. She could get as many as she wanted and she sure did! She stored these bags of quilt pieces wherever she could get them including in the old house in the holler, old cars on her property, in her own home, the green house, etc. She made some of the prettiest quilts ever seen. She owned an old Singer Peddle machine. She made lots of quilts and gave them away to family members. She was also known to give quilts to anyone she felt needed one. I can remember several times when someone stopped at the road to chat with her and a few minutes later she would go into the trailer and come out with a quilt to give them. She was never greedy and always willing to help her neighbor if she could. I was so fascinated by the old peddle sewing machine. I would sneak and pump the peddle with my feet just as fast as I could while she wasn't looking! I don't think it harmed the way it operated since she used it over and over afterward. She never said anything to me about it so I assumed it was harmless! In fact, I don't ever remember her spanking me as she did my dad and his siblings and cousins. She usually just talked to me about things. She was always very understanding and never raised her voice with me at all. Mind you, she didn't care to raise her voice to other adults if they happen to make her mad.

The Appalachian Quilt Trail is a popular trail that leads visitors across

Tennessee with more than 300 stops of agriculture, art, history, and cultural points. This trail is marked by colorful painted quilt blocks that celebrate Appalachia's historic farms, local businesses, farmer's markets, shops, and local venues. You may find yourself on unexplored back roads that lead to some interesting places. Hancock County has a variety of quilt block stops including Elrod Falls in Sneedville, River Place on the Clinch in Kyles Ford, and several barns along the route. Each quilt block contains a different pattern. Maps can be obtained to guide one through a particular trail. Quilt making was an art common to most households in Appalachia. Quilts were also hung on walls as decorations or to keep the cold out and often used to spread on the ground for a picnic.

Dad had to drive Grandma to Maryland one time after Gale's (Rob & Trish's mom) aunt had passed away. This was a Catholic family so they held a reception after the funeral to celebrate the life of the deceased. Grandma was enjoying talking with the family/friends she knew and she was drinking "tea" from the drink bar. She thought the tea was so good that she kept going back for more. When they got ready to leave, Dad and the others realized she was drunk! They ended up having to take her back to the motel so she could lie down. I had never known of her ever being a drunk. She would occasionally give us Jack Daniels Whiskey (a tablespoon) mixed with rock candy whenever we had a cold. The rock candy helped the strong drink to have a sweeter and more tolerable taste. It seemed to help our ailments. I loved the rock candy so much that I would sneak into the kitchen and get a handful from the box that was put away in the cabinet. I ate it before grandma found out! She always kept the whiskey put out of our reach. It was a good thing or we may have ended up drunk ourselves!

One time, the children told Grandma someone had been picking on them on the school bus. Fred Helton was the bus driver. Grandma got on the bus one morning herself once the children had gotten on. She told the kids if they didn't stop picking on her grandchildren, she would get her shot gun and stop them herself. Apparently, they were never picked on again and nothing was ever said about Grandma's threat. Fred Helton joked about this for years afterward. People liked grandma but at the same time, they knew not to mess with her. Mountain people can be your best friend or your enemy and if treated unfairly just one time, we will most likely forgive you but "we ain't got no use fer yee again". In mountain words, we'd "keep an eye on that snake". In other words, we won't be quick to spend any time with you if we don't have to. We are a very proud yet complex population of people with our own unique culture and dispositions that have resisted change for the last two centuries.

    Grandma had an uncle, William Henry Fletcher, who worked at Livesay Mill in the early 1900's in Kyles Ford. Henry grew up on Fox Branch Road (possibly the land or near the land my Grandmother Ethel inherited) so he later married Tom Livesay's sister, Almira. This was well before my time but the story comes from the Fletcher side of the family. The mill was located in what we always referred to as "Chris Livesay Curve" just across from the Clinch River within a mile of where the River Place on the Clinch is now. This river would flood on occasion so the family would nail bottle caps on the doorpost in the mill to mark how high the water levels went. The worst flood that ever came to the area that Grandma Ethel would have remembered was in 1977. Grandma Ethel used to visit the Livesay Mill in Rogersville Tennessee to purchase flour and meal and some of the same family ran the Kyles Ford mill. The Kyles Ford mill had shut down in 1906 (before her time) after an explosion that killed Tom's brother, Anderson. Two other men, Elijah Catron, and Henry Hurd, were visiting the mill during the explosion and were also killed. Tom was nearly cut in half and his father, Lark, was injured as well. Fortunately, Tom survived even though doctors in Rogersville predicted he would not. Henry had taken the day off to take a neighbor across the mountain to Rogersville. A belt running the saw had come off so Tom cut the steam so he could fix it. All of a sudden the steam engine exploded and the sound could be heard for miles. As the story was told, Henry and Almira lived at the Livesay Mill for a year at a time so Henry could work there and help his brother-in-law Tom. When they were not living at the mill they moved to their farm not too far from the mill towards Compromise Church. Henry taught school at Compromise Church when he was not working at the mill. He was said to be self-educated and very good with math calculations. Compromise Church was named after several members said they were going to have to "compromise" on the church name because of disagreement on what it would be called. This disagreement nearly caused the church to split. My Aunt Diana took me to VBS at Compromise as I remember turning a KFC bucket into a storage container by adding strips of pasted paper to it that later hardened. Anyway, Henry also served as Postmaster of the Kyles Ford area in 1913 and he rode a horse and delivered the mail. When it came time for the Sears and Roebuck catalogs to be delivered, the mail carriers would have to cut the straps and let them float in the river because they were so heavy. The house that sits right next to Compromise Church was a Sears and Roebuck kit and shipped in by a train. I always thought this house was a beautiful castle or mansion each time we passed by it on our way to Rogersville. There is a mountain spring located on the Kyles Ford side of Compromise where many folks went to get their water. Many families did not have running water in their homes and some still do not. Families with no running water take their old milk jugs or other containers to the spring to collect water in and take them back home to use. A white PVC pipe still sticks out of the side of the mountain and it is the best drinking water around!

Harold Owens with Robert & Patricia

You Can Take the Girl Out of the Mountains But You Cannot take the Mountains Out of the Girl

Jennifer Kinsler

4 IN THE MOUTAINS WITH GRANDMA

My dad and mom moved into the green house shortly after Papaw Paul moved out. I was probably about five years old. I often spent time with Grandma while living there and later stayed with her almost full time when I wasn't going to school. My Dad's mother, Betty, died when I was only four years old. Grapes were my favorite fruit when I was a young child. My grandmother Betty would often bring me grapes and grape bubble gum when she visited. She rode the county transportation bus along with several others to get to work across the mountain each day. Several of the women on the bus noticed she was having a hard time getting on. She could barely lift her legs up to step into the bus. The ladies told her she should go have a doctor check to see what was wrong. She was a very hard worker and determined to keep working instead of taking time to schedule an appointment. She finally became so ill she had no choice but to find out what was wrong. She was diagnosed with Scleroderma and there was not a cure nor a medicine that could treat it at the time. The disease caused her to become bed ridden so she lost use of her arms and legs. She was only forty-eight years old when she passed away. She was buried on my birthday so the family had to later come home to have a birthday party for me despite their grief. I always had two birthday cakes as my papaw Paul made sure of this. There are plenty of old Polaroid photos showing my birthday parties at the green house and other places.

The year was about 1986, so I would have been ten to eleven years old at that time. I lived with my dad (at my choice) in the green house in Kyles Ford after he and my mother divorced. As I recall, my mother had a hard time from the time my brother, Randall Jr, was born. He began having seizures at six months of age. Once doctors were finally able to find out exactly what was causing this, he had to have a shunt tube placed into his brain to keep the fluid drained off through his kidneys. A neurosurgeon, Dr. Nichols, was able to figure out what was going on. The first time I saw Randall Jr. have one of his seizures, I was very scared. His eyes rolled back into his eye sockets and his frail body tremored for several minutes. I'd never seen anything like this. The doctors back then told my parents that my brother would probably not live to be ten to eleven years old. However, he is still living today at the age of thirty-four. He continues to live with my dad as we were once told his IQ was similar to that of a seven year old child when he was in his twenties and he wasn't capable of taking care of himself. I can remember living in the green house and being in the bedroom near the back of the house with the door closed. I could hear my dad and mom arguing and talking about divorcing. I peered through the peep hole in the door so I could see them. I cried so hard when I heard them say they were planning to divorce. Divorce is very hard on children. My mother kept the other two children, Jessica and Randall, Jr, with her as my youngest sister, Chastity, had not been born yet. I later went back to live with my mother just before I married at the age of fifteen. While Dad and I were living in the green house, he had to go to work, so I stayed with Grandma Ethel during the day. Dad was a police officer at the jail in Sneedville during the term of Sheriff Gene Gibson. Grandma and I had the best times. She owned an old green Dodge Aspen so we would drive all over Fox Branch, Panther Creek, and sometimes into Sneedville and other towns in this old car. We often visited with what seemed like every single person who lived in the area. I later came to realize she was related to most of these people so that is why she visited in order to sit and talk. If there were children my age, I'd be out playing with them. Children actually went outside to play during those days. We did not have cell phones, computers, video games, nor were we interested in what was playing on television when we could be outside playing with our friends. We played with sticks, rocks, and whatever else we could find to make things fun. When we visited Grandma's Brothers Edgar and Woodrow on Panther Creek, I'd be out playing in Edgar's old car with cousins Chad, Jody, and Tonya. We pretended we could drive so we would all load into the old parked car and take a pretend trip to somewhere we imagined to go. Each of us would take turns being the "driver". We would also play in the barn with tobacco sticks or on the hay. At any given time, most elder women prepared enough food to feed their large families or just in case neighbors may stop by to eat. They were always thoughtful towards one another. Edgar's wife, Arkie, would cook all sorts of food so we enjoyed sitting at the table to eat! She probably cooked enough food to last all week or so it seemed. She was one of the best cooks around! Woodrow did not like spaghetti when Arkie cooked it. He thought it was worms so he would not eat it! Edgar and Arkie took care of Woodrow and for the longest time I was afraid of Woodrow because I thought he looked kinda scary. Grandma assured me he was harmless. He had false teeth so he would stick them out at us. I thought that was pretty scary for someone to stick their teeth out. I sure could not spit mine out like that! Once I got used to being around him, he was a lot of fun. He loved politics and had a collection of old election buttons that advertised the candidate running for the position. He kept most of the family grave yards mowed. Grandma did not like anyone picking on Woodrow as he was slightly mentally challenged. He was also easily taken advantage of. One time, some of the children went up to the graveyard (Johnson Cemetery) to play. It was there Woodrow's headstone was discovered with his name engraved so the kids came running back down the hill as fast as they could yelling "Woodrow's dead"! He had only pre-purchased his headstone years before he passed away. Many people did this in order to not place that burden on others and to have all their own arrangements taken care of. It was quite hilarious when the children found out he was still alive!

Sometimes, we would go up the road to Nora's so the kids would just continue playing in the yard. Nora was Grandma Ethel's brother Edgar's daughter. Chad, Tonya, and Jody were Nora's grandchildren and most of the time were there to play with. We always had the best of times keeping one another entertained. I remember several times going into the fields across from Nora's to play. There have been all sorts of Indian arrowheads found in this field. One of the relatives has a collection of them along with the Indian tomahawk that was passed down from generation to generation. Occasionally, we would hear Grandma and Nora talking about old times. I just wish I had remembered more and written it all down. It gets hard to trace family history once those with the information have passed on. The oral stories were the best. This is why I write things down now. I wasn't too interested when I was younger but I wish I had been!

I can also remember taking trips with Grandma to the bread and bakery store and stopping by the sewing factory to pick up more quilt pieces. Every once in a while we would go to Ed Roberts store in Virginia. This was just an old time mom and pop type country store that sold basic necessities. Ed always sat on the bench inside the store near the window. His wife, Nola, sat behind the desk where she would calculate purchases bought. She never had a cash register or even a calculator that I can remember. She would write down the cost for each item purchased on the back of a brown paper bag. Once she had all the prices written down, she would total them in her head and let you know how much you owed. All the items were bagged into this poke (mountain word for bag). Then, you were able to use your brown paper bag, or poke, as your receipt. They kept their cash in an old cigar box that sat behind the counter on a shelf. I always loved getting ice cream from this store. I can still remember the old ice cream freezer with the sliding lid.

Grandma lived less than a mile from Baker's Grocery, which was another old country store run by Carl and Edith (Tina or Teen) Baker. This store was a little more technically updated than Roberts' store as they actually used a cash register. Baker's was located just off the highway and near the Fox Branch Road turn. My dad and his siblings/cousins visited this store many times themselves. Dad and Mom said when I was just a toddler and didn't get my way, I'd fall to the ground and start pulling my hair and banging my head. I did this when I didn't get what I wanted from Baker's store. Sometimes, Cousin Stacy would come from Church Hill for a visit so we would get to walk down the road to Baker's to get snacks, sodas, and other items. Mountain folk called sodas "dope" back in those days. We collected old glass Coke or Pepsi bottles so we could take them to Baker's to sell. We had a little red wagon and the empty wooden store crates that held the bottles. We would pull the wagon down the highway to Baker's. We used the money from selling back the bottles to buy our snacks. No one ever attempted to bother us when we walked to the store or other areas. It was much safer for children to be walking on the highways/hills in those times compared to how it is today. Neighbors were nice enough to look out for each other's children. The people who lived in Kyles Ford were among a very tight knit community. Baker's sold stick bologna that Carl would slice on his meat slicer once you let him know how many pieces you wanted. This made the best bologna sandwich! I always liked JFG mayonnaise and fresh sliced garden mater (tomato) on mine. I also like my bologna fried from time to time. I have added BBQ potato chips to my fried bologna sandwich and ate it that way. We learned real quick to be creative with food while in the mountains. If you wanted a Tony's pizza, Carl could bake one in the small oven for you. Once it was baked, it would be placed back into the box it came out of for you to take with you. The store carried round life savers suckers with a hole in the middle in different flavors. My favorite were the blueberry cream ones. I can remember buying shredded bubble gum in packs that resembled a pouch of tobacco with a picture of a person in a baseball cap and shirt on the outside. We would pretend we were getting a big "chew" of tobacco! Many older folks chewed tobacco in those days so we must have thought we were mimicking them. The shredded bubble gum can still be purchased today but I have yet to find the lifesaver suckers.

Baker's also carried plastic face masks for Halloween. Back then, we didn't dress up like kids do now with all the blood and gore. Halloween was a harmless and fun event for us. We would have a mask on our face with a matching plastic cape and pants over us when we went door to door to get candy. I can remember the clown, monkey, and little ghost costumes as they didn't really look too scary. Baker's Grocery eventually shut down sometime after I moved away to another town.

Just below Baker's Grocery on the highway lived Dez Mabe and her two mentally challenged sons, David and Ronnie. Grandma often visited with them or took Dez to town when she needed to go. Dez couldn't drive so they mainly walked to get where they needed to go. Dez always had snuff in her mouth and it ran down her chin as she rarely kept it cleaned off. Ronnie was a pretty big guy but David was the shorter of the two. Most people were afraid of Ronnie and David as they were known to threaten anyone who messed with their momma or each other. No doubt their size had something to do with scaring people away. Ronnie could drink an entire jug of milk in one setting. When his milk ran out, Ronnie would walk up the road to Baker's and buy another gallon. Sometimes, I'd walk with him if I was there. He had a big jolly laugh and it was often unclear what he said when he talked. Sometimes, Dez would have to tell us what he had said. I enjoyed sitting with Ronnie and David as grandma and Dez sat and talked. Ronnie had the biggest smile. He wore overall's that would not button on the sides due to his large side. David and Dez passed away later on leaving Ronnie to himself. Someone had to take him in and care for him since he wasn't quite capable of caring for himself. The people who took care of him put him on a diet and he lost a lot of weight. Tina Baker had a picture hanging up in her store of Ronnie after his weight loss and he looked like a completely different person! I never did get to see Ronnie again.

When we were not going to Ed Roberts, Baker's store, or visiting, we were in the trailer enjoying grandma's cooking. She made the best cooked cabbage. It always made the house stink, however. She raised chickens so we often had fried chicken, chicken and dumplings, chicken on a piece of loaf bread, etc. She was known to give people in the community chickens at no charge if they needed them. Grandma killed her own chickens so I was able to help with cleaning them from time to time. She would go out in the yard and grab the chicken she wanted to kill. Then, she would wring its neck and place it on the "chopping block" which was just an old cinder block. She would take an axe and chop off the chicken's head. I usually stayed inside and watched her do this from the kitchen window. After the chicken flopped all over the place for a bit with no head, it would be brought into the trailer to prep for cooking. I recall the smell of that chicken after she boiled water to pour over it to make it easier to pluck the feathers out. I am not sure which was worse, the cabbage or the scalded chicken! My job was to pluck out the feathers one by one until they were all off. Grandma would cut the chicken up into pieces for frying/cooking/freezing. This was the best chicken because there were no additives and we always knew what they were eating since we helped scatter chicken feed on the ground for them. She kept an old freezer in the living room that was filled with beef, chicken, and other items. She always kept a brown paper type freezer wrap that she used to wrap the meat in. Freezer tape was used to hold it intact to store it for a later meal.

The chickens would often roost in the barn across from the green house. Grandma had corner areas built where they nested and laid their eggs. I loved to gather the eggs when the hens were not around. The hens might flog you if you stole their eggs while they were sitting on them or even near for that matter. We had to be very careful when collecting eggs. I loved to eat sausage and eggs cooked together. Little did I know the "sausage" was possum brains on occasion! Grandma told me later on in life what I had eaten. I always thought the "sausage" with the eggs was delicious. Sometimes, grandma would put several eggs in her incubator in order to hatch doodles (baby chicks). She kept them in her bedroom. It often took about twenty-one days for the baby chicks to grow and hatch. I was able to keep watch on them through the glass dome lid. Sometimes, one could be seen pecking away at the shell before making its appearance. Every once in a while there would be a rotten smell from one of the babies dying before it hatched. This is most often due to the humidity problem inside the incubator or even inside the home itself. I always enjoyed watching the baby chicks with their momma. I would make up names for the baby chicks and try to follow them around outside. Once, I was flogged by a hen because I got too close to her babies! It was not too pleasant so I made sure to keep my distance afterward.

The old barn was a fun place to play. I remember being in the loft top often. I can also remember the outside being decorated with dead coon skins! Coon (raccoon) hunting was a favorite sport in our family. Raccoons were first hunted by Native Americans and later adopted by the British and European settlers. My Uncle Goob owned specialty bred dogs called coonhounds that stayed tied up at the green house. I'd help keep them fed and watered. These dogs were trained to follow the scent of a raccoon's pelt and once mastered it was taken to the woods by itself or with other dogs. Neighbors often joined in and went together thus forming the "coon club" at the old Kyles Ford School. Coon hunts would take place at night. The dogs would be turned loose to tree a raccoon (raccoon chased up a tree and dog left at the base barking). Sometimes, the dogs would get lost so the owner made sure to keep them tagged with contact information so whoever found one could call and let the owner know where they were. The coon hides would be hung on the barn to dry and later sold for their fur. Raccoon fur is used to make coonskin caps, as worn by Davy Crockett. It was also used to make clothing, coats, and the whole coon was a food source for Native American Indians.

One of the barn stables was a holding place for field corn. This was a type of hard corn that was used to feed livestock. Grandma owned several cattle so I'd get to help shell the corn off the cob and throw it to the cows at feeding time. This was a very hard job as the roughness of the shell often left blisters on my hands. It was hard to wear gloves and shell the corn. Sometimes, we fed it to the chickens. When calling for the cattle to make their way from the holler down to the barn, we had to yell "whooo", "sue-ee" or "Come Heifer"!

Robert Owens holding me
Tony Maness (Aunt Diana's husband)
The barn across from green house is in background

Kyles Ford School

Jennifer Kinsler

Me and Dad
Christmas 2015

You Can Take the Girl Out of the Mountains But You Cannot take the Mountains Out of the Girl

Jennifer Kinsler

5 SCHOOL DAYS

Going to school was something I often hated until later on. We lived a short time in a small house in Back Valley where the mental health center is now. My Kindergarten teacher wasn't very pleasant. She was scary and sometimes mean. I was sitting on a red tricycle during recess and she grabbed me by the arm and told me to "shut that crying up". Of course, I was scared since it was a new place away from my parents or anyone I knew. I had to figure out a plan to escape Kindergarten. Once I got to the gym each morning during this Kindergarten year, I thought I'd sneak out of the building and down into Sneedville, which was only a few minutes' walk. I snuck out every day until I was caught. I'd go sit along the block wall that wrapped around the courthouse until I saw the buses coming off the hill. Then, I'd walk home and pretend I'd been at school all day. Once, I even hid out in our outhouse (yard toilet) so my parents wouldn't know I was there. As soon as the bus rolled by I'd come out of the toilet and walk into the house as if I'd been to school! I made it a point to always keep watch through the cracks in the toilet walls just in case someone from the house needed to take a potty break. This would give me enough time to come out and hide until they were done. One day, I was standing at an old building at the bottom of the hill from the Hancock County Elementary School. Mattie Mills came by and stopped to ask me where my parents were. I somehow convinced her to drive me all the way to Camp's where my Grandmother Benia Mae "Nude" lived. I can't remember the exact story I told Mattie but she bought it hook, line, and sinker. I didn't sneak away from school but a few times before I was caught. I was smart enough to figure out how to get away from school but not smart enough to know I'd for sure get caught eventually. My experience with this Kindergarten teacher set the stage for the remainder of my school days/years until I ended up with some very good teachers later on who were nice and encouraged me. As far as I know, that Kindergarten teacher taught school until she retired and she treated other students the same way. She should not have been a Kindergarten teacher or perhaps a teacher at all.

Being with Grandma Ethel during those days often meant I had very few items of clothing that were in decent shape. My parents were not wealthy and Grandma did what she could to see I went to school presentable. I can remember the time I had britches (denim blue jeans) with no button so I had them tied together with a shoe string so they would stay on me. As soon as Grandma Ethel saw this, she said a few choice words about who allowed their children to wear such clothing as this. She repaired my jeans by adding a new button.

At some point during my elementary school years, wearing holes in your jeans was a new fashion trend. I didn't have any jeans with holes so I decided to make my own "holes" in the jeans I already owned. Grandma found them while I was at school one day. When I came home, she told me she had fixed my britches. She had actually taken old quilt scraps and sewed underneath the missing denim. I felt too bad to let her know this was "the style" so I just started wearing jeans that eventually became a new fashion trend! Sometimes, I was known to wear her clothes, if they fit well enough. I found a colorful sweater in her bathroom that looked like a patch work quilt. I thought the sweater was so pretty but some of my wealthier classmates did not agree. I remember being made fun of for wearing that sweater. I didn't care as I continued to wear it. I thought they were probably just jealous because they didn't have one. It was my grandmother's sweater and she was a Southern icon in my eyes.

One of my favorite things about elementary school was going to the library. The library was also my favorite place to hang out during my years at Walter's State Community College. Books seemed to provide a type of solace for me. I still love to read, especially non-fiction and historical books. Mrs. Katherine Cantwell was our elementary school librarian and she is now the Vice President of the Hancock County Historical & Genealogical Society that's located inside the old 1860 jail in Sneedville. My Dad worked at this historic jail as a deputy from 1986-88 until the new prison opened. I loved to listen to Mrs. Katherine read stories to us. The book fairs were my favorite but I didn't always have money to spend. Sometimes, Mrs. Katherine would give us a free bookmark or pencil. She was always very nice and had the sweetest smile. Our classes would occasionally get to go out front to the red reading building to watch a movie with Ms. Diane Ferguson. Our school had a hidden tunnel underneath where janitors had to keep the furnace heated with coal. The teachers would occasionally walk us through the tunnel after lunch. It was dark and scary walking through the tunnel. Just up the stairs at the end of the tunnel was a closet where we could stop to purchase pencils, erasers, folders, etc. Mrs. Mattie Mills ran this as our school store. She would often give pencils to the students who did not have money to buy them. I remember many times standing behind students who had money to purchase something when I didn't but Mrs. Mattie always noticed. She would give us a pencil at no charge and tell us not to tell anybody. During our school ice cream suppers (fundraiser with no ice cream!), the tunnel would be used for haunted houses. Those were some fun times!

One morning, I was getting ready for school at Grandma's. I had just washed my hair so I bent over to dry it upside down. Drying your hair upside down somehow made it look better and fuller. I was being silly moving around with the hair dryer. I accidentally walked backward out the back door and landed myself on a sharp pointed rock that went into my lower back. That was painful. Grandma had to get a hold of my dad. He came and took me to the ER in Sneedville where I had to have several stitches. I think this may be why I have always had lower back pain. I still dry my hair upside down on occasion with the exception of trying to walk out a door!

Fred Helton was still the same bus driver on the branch as when my Dad rode the bus to school. Each morning, I had to watch for the bus to come up near the Lillie House to have time to stand at the road as the bus came by to pick me up. This was an old shack on the side of the road below Grandma's where the pear tree was. Lillie Nichols lived in a house right across from this shack but it is no longer there. Some people use to claim that the Lillie House was haunted. The house had deteriorated pretty badly and the window glass was missing. Dad had a cousin who use to get inside the house with a white jacket on and wave his arms up and down making people think they saw a Ghost! Anyway, Fred's bus was often late getting to school since he had to come all the way from the third district where he lived. Students were never considered late as it wasn't their fault, however. We could eat a late breakfast when all the other children had gone on to class. Fred was a character. He had a bad habit of hunching his shoulder up as he drove. I am not sure why. He often found it entertaining to pair students up whom he thought would "make a good match". He tried to pair me up with a guy named Lee but I was never interested in Lee. He pulled this stunt on others too but I can't ever remember it working out between any of them either. He just thought he was a matchmaker! Riding Fred's bus was one thing but missing the bus was often adventurous. Uncle Rob had to load me up into his Dodge truck and pretty much chase the bus down to Panther Creek or sometimes all the way into Sneedville. Fred usually saw us so he would stop long enough to allow me to get on. Some days, I would have rather been at home with Grandma instead of sitting in a classroom all day or riding that bus. Grandma was a lot more fun and interesting! Some of the older girls on the bus liked to make fun of me. Most of the time, it was the clothing I wore. In my case, I had very little clothing to wear. My husband and I always taught our girls to never make fun of someone because of the clothing they wore as it may have been all they had. Our girls were good at picking out other children they felt needed clothes by digging into their own closets and taking those to them.

    Grandma always kept strawberry candy that even had a wrapper that resembled little strawberries. This fascinated me! I took some of it to school a few times so I could sell it and make some money. I kept the candy in a green metal box with a lid that belonged to grandma. It was shaped like an old lunch box but smaller. In elementary school, we had to sit in the gym in the mornings before school took up for the day. It was during this time I thought I'd sell my candy. I sold it for .5cents each. I sold quite a bit of it. I am not sure if Grandma ever missed any of it as she always kept plenty in stock. I remember giving away some of the money I earned once to Gina Reed. Her father was our town doctor in addition to Dr. Pierce. Her face lit up like a light bulb! I felt good about giving her my money because it made her feel good. I can't remember if I gave any more of it away but I soon stopped selling candy.

Uncle Goob and Cousin Rob liked to aggravate me. They thought they would sneak and get my money jar that I had hid. We were outside in the front yard of the green house one day and they started throwing my money jar back and forth saying "Look what we found, we can go buy us something now." Boy was I mad! That was mine and I wanted it back. I wrestled between the both of them until I eventually got so upset I started to punch them. They realized I was real mad so they stopped playin' around and gave me my money jar. They were quite the characters.

    One time I needed money to pay for my school yearbook. Instead of asking grandma for money, I just found one of her checkbooks and wrote out a check myself. I don't think I had thought about getting caught after the fact. Those were the days of receiving all your written checks back in the mail from the bank. Apparently, I had done it correctly. Cousin Trish sat me down outside her back door steps one day and talked to me about taking something that didn't belong to me. She also told me all I had to do was ask and someone would have paid for my yearbook. She told me I must never do this again, so I didn't. I can't remember why I never asked for the money. Maybe I was just fascinated with writing out a check myself or maybe I thought anyone could do it since I'd watched grandma write checks numerous times. It could have been around the time teachers were teaching us how to write out a check!

    Our class had a speech writing contest. I thought I'd write my speech about creation from the book of Genesis in the Holy Bible. The teacher had taught us to keep our notes on small index cards and to always look our audience in the eye as much as possible when talking. My speech was chosen to be given at the local high school among other contestants from different grade levels. We traveled to the high school by bus and were able to gather in the cafeteria where judges could listen to each speech. I wasn't nervous at all. When it came my turn, I proudly stood up there using my notes but trying to speak without looking down at my cards. I told a cafeteria full of people about God creating the whole world in six literal days and how it was all "good." My speech did not win, but I came in at third place and received a ribbon. I don't know what ever happened to my ribbon. Grandma probably put it up somewhere and forgot about it.

There were two "Bible ladies" as we called them that would come into our classroom on occasion to teach us Bible stories- Ms. Cora Robinson and Ms. Velma Giddings. These ladies taught Bible stories when my dad was in school also. They were the nicest ladies. They brought in huge felt boards with felt Bible characters and placed the characters on the board as they told each story. Then, they would sing songs and teach us those songs. One of the songs was "Fishers of Men". It was about how Jesus could make us fishers of men that could share the gospel with others in hopes they would come to know Christ as their personal savior. Sometimes, they would sing the songs before the lesson. They had a way of making Bible stories come to life. They would teach us a Bible verse and, in turn, we had to remember it. They often told us to "hide God's word in our hearts". They would give each of the students their own personal New Testament, which was a little red Bible containing the New Testament and Psalms from the Old Testament. This could have been the reasoning behind my Genesis speech. The ladies held a Summer Bancroft Bible Camp and children could attend each week. I was never able to go to this but many others were. Some even told that the two ladies would come to their homes and teach them the Bible. I've even heard of these missionary ladies traveling to neighboring towns to teach in various schools, camps, etc. These women had an impact on many children who grew up to tell about it. They had an impact on my life as well. I continue to love reading the Bible. At some point, the Bible ladies were no longer allowed to come into our schools to teach the Bible stories. Apparently, it was too offensive to someone. There is no way our public schools today would allow Bible teachers to come into the classrooms and teach Bible lessons. Back then, the Bible did not offend people unless they were not living it. This is the problem for most of today's youth. In a sense, we threw God out of school to do our own thing and now we see the consequences of it. Things are now being taught in schools that are false, such as dinosaurs existing before humans and billions of years of earth's existence. The Bible just doesn't back this up.

Sometimes, in the afternoons after school, Grandma and I would sit on the couch to watch television. She did not have cable so there were only a few channels to watch. She used an outdoor antennae or rabbit ears to broadcast the few channels that came on. Grandma loved country music as well as gospel so we often watched Hee Haw. This was an American television show that featured country music with a twist of humor. The show aired from 1969-1971 followed by twenty years of reruns. It was very popular during the 1980's. Hee Haw was hosted by Buck Owens and Roy Clark and featured characters such as Grandpa Jones, Minnie Pearl, Gordie Tapp, and Lulu Roman. It stayed on for about an hour and different country music stars often made their appearance such as Dolly Parton, Porter Wagner, Tennessee Ernie Ford, Archie Campbell from Bulls Gap Tennessee, The Mandrell sisters, Johnny Cash, George Jones, and many others. The jokes often told on Hee Haw were rather corny but mountain folk could relate to the hillbilly culture of the show. The word Hee-Haw means the bray of a donkey or a loud rude laugh. The show featured a cartoonish donkey with a wide open mouth that spit out "Hee Haw" at the end of the show's farewell. Hee Haw remains a beloved and popular show that can now be purchased on DVD boxed sets. Some other shows we enjoyed were Andy Griffith, The Dukes of Hazard, and The Beverly Hillbillies. I still watch these shows today.

Grandma had an antique 8 track tape player so she often played country, bluegrass, or gospel music. Children these days would have no idea what an 8 track tape is. I think my dad still has several tapes of his own along with a player to listen to them. I first learned to sing "My Golden Shoes" from an 8 track tape which contained a gospel song by a local group called the Duck Creek Quartet. I also liked another song called "Dreaming of a Little Cabin". While we were not listening to gospel we could be heard singing the old time country. I feel the old time country songs from back then are much better than the modern ones today. The music was decent for the most part and the whole family could enjoy it. The group called Alabama with Ronnie Owens was one of my all-time favorite country music bands. I liked to pretend we were related to Ronnie because that was Grandpa Marvin's last name too. It's possible we could be related but I've never tried to figure that out. Alabama songs like "Mountain Music" and "Song of the South", "Dixieland Delight" and "Tennessee River" were songs mountain people could relate to and it made them feel good. There was nothing like riding down an old dusty river road with the windows rolled down blaring Alabama's music. Our voices could be heard singing along and it echoed in the hills. If my mountains could speak, my at the stories they could tell!

Sometimes, we would get to go to the old Green Top Inn down in Sneedville. This was located at the corner where the Corner Mart is now.

They served good ole' country cookin'. They made the best cornbread! They often had local bands that came to play music so we could sit and listen to them sing as we enjoyed our meal. Grandma took my dad and his siblings/cousins there when they were younger.

Jim Trent occasionally hosted public dances at the local Sneedville Community Center. The dances were often held at the Farmer's Market building below the elementary school before they started having them at the Community Center. (By this time I was a little older so I had gone back to stay with mom in the mobile home park behind Greene's Supermarket in Sneedville. We lived right next door to the prison where dad worked. During this time, I could see through the prison fence and often watched or waved to the inmates from my back yard.) While at the community center dances, Jim had his musical setup with a disco ball and lights. He played soundtracks or possibly records. I could cut quite a rug in those days! To "cut a rug" is a synonym or idiom for dancing. We could request certain songs be played and even have the song dedicated to another person there. One time, an older, good looking guy from out of town dedicated "Every Rose has its Thorn" by Poison to me and asked me to slow dance. He breathed down the back of my neck the whole time. That was the first and last time I ever saw him. I never really understood the message to me in that song or his annoying breathing. Maybe he was just a lonely old coot having memories of some other girl. Anyway, those dances were so much fun. I know I tormented my poor Dad begging him to let me go.

The first real boyfriend I had was during my sixth grade year. A new male student had just transferred from Florida and he took notice of me out of all the other girls in school. They were so jealous and it made me feel pretty good. We held hands walking through the elementary school tunnel. We met up at the local pool hall, ice-cream suppers, and talked for hours over the telephone. In those days, the telephones had curled cords that would not stretch very far throughout the house so it often meant sitting near an adult who could listen to every word said. He was also the very first boy I ever kissed. There was an old building beside the town pool hall that left room for an alley way in between these two buildings. We often walked through this alley way to get to the other side quicker instead of walking all the way around a couple of buildings. My boyfriend and I were in the alley when my first kiss happened! How exciting for me as a young girl. At least exciting until my Uncle Goob drove by and yelled "Is that you, Jennifer"! So, off I ran as fast as I could go until I reached the trailer park where I lived. The new prison was being constructed during this time so I fell over some cinder blocks and skinned my knees up pretty good. By the time I got to our trailer, there was my uncle to tell my mom he had caught me kissing a boy in town! It was just an innocent kiss. That boy's family moved back to Florida within a year or so. Instead of telling me they were moving, he decided to write a farewell letter and send it by my cousin Myshone. I cried for days. I never saw him again until years passed by. I was already married by the time he came back looking for me. Mountain girls don't sit around waiting so I had several boyfriends after him before I met and fell in love with Shannon. Shannon was my first true love and still is. I fell in love with Shannon during my eighth grade year. He did not like me, at first. The first time I ever saw him was near the creek at my Aunt Diana's house. Her son Dougie was just a baby so I carried him down to the creek to play. I was in my two piece bikini so we could get in the water. I believe this was the coldest water in the entire county. All of a sudden out of nowhere came this handsome guy walking across the creek from the work field side. He had been helping my Uncle Tony put up hay. He stopped to ask me if I knew where Tony was. I told him he was up at the house. We had some mutual friends, Robbie & Sharon, who tried to hook us up later. Robbie lived just over the hill from Aunt Diana's so he and Shannon were best friends throughout school. Shannon asked me to the prom during my ninth grade year so I gladly accepted. I remember being jealous during eighth grade over Shannon's prom date, which wasn't me. His brother, Rodney, knew I liked Shannon. He took it upon himself to brag about Shannon taking some other girl to the prom that year. This made me mad! Shannon and I had been dating several months during my ninth grade year. He surely must have thought if I'd fight over him, I'd be worth his time! My parents could not afford an expensive dress so my step-mom Tammie and Aunt Diana took me to Morristown in search of something to wear. We ended up renting a dress from a costume rental shop called Trinkets and Treasures. It was red, covered with black lace and had a large red rose on the front. It had matching black lace gloves and we found black flats to match at the local Wal-Mart. The rental fee was only $45, which was well within our budget. Shannon and I had a wonderful time at our prom that year. Shannon wrote in his graduation memory book that I was his most special date. Grandma also seemed to like him very well. She told him to always be good to me. When we were expecting our first child, Ashley, Shannon promised Grandma Ethel that he would always take care of me and our family. She seemed to be content with that. He has kept his word. We have been married twenty-six years as of 2017. I wouldn't trade him for any man in the whole world as I feel he is a very special person! My mountains gave me my first love experiences among many other memorable events I'll cherish until the day I die.

    I attended the Hancock County High School which is now the headquarters for the Board of Education and other government offices. I could walk to the high school from the trailer park where we lived in less than five minutes. The big thing for us as teenagers was riding around town. We made the circle around the small town over and over until we had to go home. If we had to use the bathroom we often went up on Piss Hill. This was not what it was actually called but was where everyone went to do their business! I'd often walk to town since I lived right there in it. I didn't have my driver's license so I hitched a ride with older friends. Friends would gather and park their cars in parking lots where we could sit and talk for hours and watch as others circled by. There wasn't anything else to do in town. We had no stores other than Greene's Supermarket and no restaurants other than Hardees and Mrs. Bea's. The Green Top Inn had shut down before the Hardee's came. For a time, we had a Pizza Ria behind the courthouse that was a favorite place for all the young folks to go. They had a room near the back kitchen where we could play video game machines. My favorite game was Pac-Man. I racked up thousands of points and tried to keep my name listed on the screen for top players. When we were not at the Pizza Ria we could be found at the local Pool Hall. Here is where I learned to play pool and I often beat many of the guys. We could drop some quarters in the jukebox and play songs as we played a game of pool or played the video game machines. Grandma always told me to not let anyone run over me (pick on me and do nothing about it). I was walking down the hall one day at our high school and I saw Shannon with his head poking out of Home Economics room. I smiled at him and may have said hello. There was a new girl who had moved into town standing next to him at the door. For whatever reason, she thought she would call me a bitch once I was past the door. She may have liked Shannon also or they may have dated. Just as the first bell rang signaling for us to be in class in a few minutes, I stopped and turned to look at this girl. "Just you wait, I'll get you" were my exact words. I knew she also walked home like I did so I waited until I was off school grounds so I would not get into trouble. I waited for her at the bridge near the creek just before the sewage plant. I don't think she thought I was serious as she came bouncing down the road happy with all smiles. I told her to never again call me a bitch. I grabbed her and we both rolled down the hill towards the creek. I had a good grip on her head as we rolled over and over and the next thing I remember was Mr. Norman Greene separating us. He was my favorite eighth grade teacher. Mr. Greene had stopped the after school traffic including all the school buses and parked his truck in the middle of the road so he could get out and stop our fight. We were not on school grounds so we never got into trouble for fighting. I saw this girl many years later after we were adults so we exchanged our hello's and smiles in a rather nice way as each of us asked the other how we had been. High School drama is pretty much constant. This was one of a few fights I was involved in that most often had something to do with a boy.

    I did, however, spend my fair share of days with Mrs. Polly Riley during in-school suspension. A couple of my fights took place during the school day so I had no choice but to serve time with Mrs. Polly. Mr. Gary Johnson was our high school principal. Most students were afraid of Mr. Johnson as he was firm and strict and he used a large paddle for spanking. Most were afraid of him, but not me. Some of the people in my own family were meaner than he was so I'd often tell him I wasn't going to allow anyone to be picking on me whether I had to serve time or get a paddling. I'd walk up and down the halls and Mr. Johnson often gave me that stink eye look of letting me know I'd best stay out of trouble. I just gave him my look right back of don't be looking at me like that. Mrs. Polly was another firm and strict teacher. She didn't care to yell at you, tell you to shut up, or use choice words to get her point across. I liked Mrs. Polly. She was always nice to me because I never gave her any trouble and I always did my work. We had to sit in her class as punishment and do work the entire school day. We weren't even allowed to eat lunch with our other classmates. She would occasionally tell us stories about her grandbabies. Little Dennis Collins was one who stayed in trouble all the time and gave Mrs. Polly the hardest time. He called her a bitch one day in class. She gave him a piece of her mind and told him to never call her a bitch again. Dennis lived up on Newman's Ridge (Melungeon ridge) now called Johnson ridge and he rode the same school bus I did. He was always nice to me as Grandma often visited them and gave their family chickens, quilts and such. They would also stop to see Grandma from time to time.

Green Top Inn.
Mrs. Bea's Restaurant next door

The Hancock County Elementary School before it was torn down for the new one to be built.

The Hancock County High School building.

Jennifer Kinsler

«You Can Take the Girl Out of the Mountains But You Cannot take the Mountains Out of the Girl»

6 MEMORABLE MOMENTS

There are some things a person never forgets as long as they live. These memories are almost always special or interesting enough to be easy to recall. I've had many memorable moments growing up in my mountains. Among these were the fishing trips we often took around the Kyles Ford area. There are so many great things about fishing, such as learning how to fish to catch your supper for the night or learning which hole is the best for fishing. The greatest by far is creating memories with the people we love. I could sit around for days and tell of all our fishin' stories. One in particular started out as Cousin Stacy and I would go beside Grandma's barn to dig the worms, or "night crawlers" as some would call them. The dirt there was rich with cow manure and black as coal soot but produced the best and biggest worms for fishin'. We have also fished with corn kernels, chicken livers, and dough balls. Dough balls are simply the white section from a piece of loaf bread rolled into a ball. Once we gathered enough bait for our trip we would head out to the river bank. A few spots we enjoyed most were on the Clinch River. Cherokee Indians hunted and fished along the Clinch River prior to the arrival of pioneer settlers. This river is also home to many vulnerable animal species including more than 30 varieties of rare freshwater mussels and 19 species of fish. In the past, these mussels often contained fresh water pearls that could be used to make buttons, knife handles, pistol grips, or used as chicken feed. Sometimes, we would find a tightly closed shell that we would pry open with our fingers to see a live mussel inside but we never found any pearls. Tennessee River pearls were designated the state gem of Tennessee. During the late 1800's to early

1900's, mountain folks searched mussels for these pearls to make extra money to support their families. They would take them to the local stores to sell. They are among the most beautiful and durable pearls in the world. The shells were valuable as well. There was a controversial issue over the construction of the new Kyles Ford Bridge because of the endangered mussels that lived beneath it. It is now illegal to get these mussels out of the river. If caught, one will pay a hefty fine or possibly serve jail time. The basin of the Clinch River has been identified as the number one hotspot in the US for imperiled aquatic species. One of our fishin' spots in particular was right behind the old Wallen's Grocery, which is now River Place on the Clinch. Mrs. Katherine Wallen Cantwell's father ran this old store prior to its closing and becoming vacant. It was later sold to the Willis family but was never reopened by them. Clinch Powell RC&D purchased it from the Willis' and opened up the new restaurant and general store. (River Place is unique in that it has a restaurant, general store, lodging, and canoeing. They feature live music by local and regional performers on the back deck every weekend throughout the year.) This area also had its own post office that was established in 1871 and discontinued in 1997. I still remember the old Walter Willis gas station where we could pick up mail and get gas/snacks after the original post office located next door had closed. We could see the Edward R. Talley Bridge directly in front of us from the bank of the river as we fished. This old historic bridge was built in 1927-28. It was originally built as a toll bridge that crossed the Clinch River in the north part of Hancock County and was one of three bridges like this still in existence until 2015. After the bridge's rapid deterioration it had to be shut down for a new one to be constructed. The old bridge was sand blasted, painted, closed off at each end, and remains there as a historic icon in the community. Not too far down from the bridge was the baptizing hole. Church members gathered there to baptize new believers and this still continues today because the property owner made it a point to include this practice in the contract with The Tennessee Nature Conservancy who started working there to figure out ways to keep the river healthy and the mussels protected. This was no easy task to talk mountain folk into working with anyone they deemed to be from the "government". Trust is something outsiders have to earn from the mountain people. It was also not easy for the people of the mountain when they learned the new bridge had to be constructed to replace the old. Those going outside the county had to take lengthy detours for nearly three years during the construction of the new one.

But, getting back to fishing, most often, someone who had been to our particular fishing spot near the bridge before we came had left their handmade fishing pole holder, or stake. Sometimes we had to search for the right type of tree branch or sticks to make our own holders so we would leave them for the next fisherman. The stick had to have a two pronged section shaped like a V at the top with the bottom section as long as your arm. These holders had to be stuck in the ground deep enough so they could keep our fishing pole steady until we got a hit (fish bite). This kept us from having to hold our fishing pole in our hands the whole time. We just had to make sure to keep an eye on our pole as the fish could very well pull it into the river. We have been known to make our own fishing poles out of a stick or reed by attaching a string and hook. If the fish didn't seem to be biting that day we would move on down the river to another location. One time we stopped at a familiar place to fish. The adults picked out their spot so Cousin Stacy and I went on up the bank to find our own spot away from the adults. It was here we felt she could have nearly drowned. She lost her balance and one of her feet slid into the edge of the river. The next thing I heard was "help, help"! If I hadn't been there to pull her back up, there is no telling the outcome of that story. She was glad I was there and so was I.

When we were not able to go fishin' on the river banks, we just fished off the bridge in front of the green house. We would stretch out on our stomachs across a section of the bridge while hanging our arms/hands over it enough to teeter our fishing pole with hook and bait into the creek. We snagged creek minners' (minnows) or the occasional crawdad (crayfish). Grandma used to tell us we "best not" let one of those old crawdads get ahold of our fingers or it would "not let go til lightnin' struck!" We had no interest in a crawdad being stuck to our fingers that long so we would sling our pole back and forth while striking the line against the water or bank to make them "fall off"! We would catch the crawdads by using jars/cups to get them to back into without picking them up with our hands. We were told the same outcome also applied to a snapping turtle if you allowed it to get a hold of your finger so we sometimes caught one by using a big five gallon bucket.

Grandma was equipped with old wives tales so we heard our fair share of them. According to one definition, an Old wives' tale is an epithet used to indicate that a supposed truth is actually a superstition or something untrue, to be ridiculed. It can also be said sometimes that old wives tales are a type of urban legend, said to be passed down by older women to a younger generation. Grandma told us we better wear shoes outside or we would get worms from the ground. We didn't worry about such things until I had a ringworm come up on my leg. I was up the road at Cousin Trish's house when she saw it she told me I had to be treated. All the children present had to take a pill, according to Dr. Reed. A ringworm isn't actually a worm at all but a skin infection that can be caught from another person, a pet, fungus, or from the soil. Mine was round, itchy, and red with the inside section clear liquid like snot. I hated the thought of worms in my skin! Also around the same time the sky darkened in mid-day and a swarm of locusts zoomed over our heads. We had no idea what had just happened. They were so loud we had to cover our ears and stoop towards the ground until they passed by. They came like clouds and we never saw them again after that. We were treated for the ringworm and never had them again either.

When I was twelve years old, Grandma and I went to spend a week with her sister, Jeanette Johnson Eaton, who lived in Jonesborough. They lived in a huge, white, two story farmhouse. I loved this house as it had such a country charm to it. Grandma and I slept upstairs in a bed that was so high we had to use a step stool to climb in it. I went to use the bathroom and noticed bright red blood on the tissue paper. I was literally scared to death! I went to Grandma and told her something was wrong with me. After I told her "what" was wrong, Aunt Jeanette said to her "Lord, Ethel, haven't you ever told that youngin' about the birds and the bees?" Of course, I was thinking about the birds and bees that fly and buzz around outside. What could I possibly not know about bees since I had been stung several times or birds of all sorts with as many as I had seen? It was then I was sat down at the kitchen table with Grandma and Aunt Jeanette to learn about the facts of life and what happens after. I was told I could never get in any water while menstruating as it might "kill me" as it once nearly killed one of their sisters who got into the creek while having hers. I later learned I would not die by taking a bath or getting in water while "Aunt Flo" came for a visit. That famous birds and bees term was accredited to John Burroughs, a naturalist who lived in the Catskill Mountains and wrote about it in a small booklet to help explain the work of nature in a easy to understand language for children. I certainly understood after their talk with me that day. Aunt Jeanette and her daughter Sandy made it a point to visit Grandma often. I always enjoyed getting to see them.

Among other memorable visits for Grandma and me were our times spent at the home of Bus and Allie Kinsler who lived just up the road. When traveling the branch you either went up or down depending on which way you were going. If you were going down the branch, you were headed to Baker's Grocery. As Grandma and Allie talked, their granddaughter, Angela, or "Ang" as we called her, and I would play. On Occasion, Angela's cousins Missy and Mylenda would be there so we would keep ourselves entertained. One particular day I decided to bicycle up the road to play with them. I somehow caught my denim shorts on the bicycle seat as I was getting off so they ripped nearly off one side of my leg exposing part of my butt cheek. All of a sudden I heard bouts of laughter coming from my playmates. Well, I did not think it to be so funny. I quickly jumped back on my bicycle and peddled just as fast as I could back down the road to Grandma's so I could change clothes. Angela was my very first playmate according to writings in an old pink baby book my parents had. Grandma Ethel kept this put up so I'd often get it out to read things about my birth and toddlerhood. I never knew what happened to this book after I left Grandma's. I assumed it was lost in her trailer somewhere.

As part of entertaining ourselves, we would walk next door to the Belchers to borrow their skateboards. They sang in a gospel group called "The Gospel Four". Down the road we went, flat on our bellies on those boards until we ran into the bank, jumped off, or had a wreck to stop ourselves. That part was rather dangerous but we were having fun. The Belchers owned a cool minivan with side seats and lights in the back. During summer, they would pick me up and take me to Vacation Bible School at Livesay's Chapel Church. Sometimes, Cousin Stacy would be there to go with me. We made all sorts of crafts focused on Bible lessons. The last night was always the fun night to enjoy food, games, and demonstrating what we had learned for the week. I always loved getting to go and I am thankful for those who made it part of their routine to include me. Later in my adult life, I was privileged to be VBS Director for four years at a church our family attended in Rogersville.

One late evening, Grandma and I were just sitting around and a guy we called Grover stopped by. He often stopped to say hello and see how Grandma was doing. However, on this particular evening, he was a bit tipsy. Grandma took his keys away from him and invited him to sleep on her couch for the night. I always slept in the bed with her so the next morning when I woke up, I had the great luxury of cleaning up his urine from the couch. I was so mad at Grandma and could not understand why she would allow this man to sleep and pee on our couch! I realized later on that she did not want him to be driving on the highway in the shape he was in. She had looked after the friend that had looked after her so many times.

At times, our visitors were not so welcome. Cousin Rob had a few friends Grandma highly disliked. She was good to everybody but these particular friends were not the best influence, or so she thought, in Rob's life. Whenever one of them happened to stop by and she could get to the door before Rob, she slammed the front door back so hard as she opened it that I thought it would certainly fall to the ground after it smashed against the side of the trailer. The next thing out of her mouth was "Get the hell out of here you damn pot heads!" So, they left...quickly. This door slamming was done many times until these influential friends started to drive by and stop farther up the road and wait. Rob would often go out to meet them and leave while Grandma cussed the whole time. Rob made some interesting friends along the way as he was a friend to anyone regardless of their personal choices. At times, they simply picked him up to go work somewhere. One guy who often stopped by had a wooden leg. We called him "Woody". Rob had another friend we called "Fried Clyde" but don't ask me why as I seriously don't know. Both guys were always nice to me and Grandma seemed to like them as well. If she liked you, you were considered to be a purdy (pretty) good guy or gal.

Rob was always a respectable guy and well-liked by everyone that knew him. I loved being around him as he was quite humorous. One day, Cousin Stacy and I were in Rob's bedroom as he was resting after a day's work. We were bored and goofing off with him. He asked us what we wanted to be when we grew up. We both told him we wanted to be country singers and make it to big Nashville, Tennessee. He asked us what we would sing but neither of us really knew. He told us he knew the perfect song and began to belt it out line by line. "Wrinkled panties, hanging down my winder (pronounced wen-dur for window)." We laughed and laughed and he told us we just might "make it to Rogersville (across the mountain) with that song"! He always encouraged us to stay in school and make something of ourselves.

Sometimes Dad and his siblings/cousins would load us all into the car and take us across the mountain to Rogersville to "The Jolly Roger Drive In" Movie Theater. We would park in the field and sit in our car to watch the big screen. I remember we had to attach the speakers on our partially rolled down car window to listen to the movie as we sat in the car. Sometimes, we could sit out on a blanket or on the back of the tailgate or hood depending on what we drove to get there. We could get popcorn and dopes (mountain word for soda pop). These outdoor drive-in theaters were soon replaced with modern indoor ones. There are still a few drive-in theaters around but they are very sparse these days. One time Dad and the others were going to take us to a carnival or fair. Cousin Stacy and I had been playing and we found a hen's nest in an old car. As Stacy began to pick up the eggs, I heard a loud pop followed by a horrible smell. Unfortunately, the egg had splattered all over her leaving her drenched in the putrid fragrance. She was told to go inside and get cleaned up before we could go to the fair but we never made it because some trouble makers came by harassing Dad and Goob.

As we stayed outside often during our childhood years, there were a few times the rain came pounding down. I can't remember if we were playing in the holler or the barn but we didn't always make it back to the trailer before getting wet. Running in the rain in flip flops or bare feet meant feeling the cool mountain mud between your toes. I'd have to take my shoes off to run better. The mud was all squishy and sometimes caused me to slip and fall as I ran with shoes on. Washing my shoes with caked on mud would stop the sink drain up if I didn't scrape it off first. Grandma's trailer did not have proper plumbing until the Sneedville Health Department notified her that she had to have a septic installed. I can remember flushing the toilet then hearing and watching the water splatter out of the long white PVC pipe that stuck out from underneath the trailer.

For many years, the waste went into the creek behind the trailer. The same creek we played in but never got sick. The green house did not have a bathroom at all. There was an outdoor toilet on top of the hill behind the house but we usually just squatted down beside the house, especially if it was dark. If we took a bath at the green house we had to heat water on the stove and just wash off with a rag (wash cloth). I can't remember ever having a heating unit in either of the homes. We used box fans during summer and a wood burning stove during winter months. You may think this would be a terrible way to live but to us this was just a way of life. As children, we didn't give it much thought.

Historic Kyles Ford Bridge

Mammaw Betty Lucas with Baby Jennifer

Cousins Stacy (left) & Mancha (holding baby doll) with me on right.

You Can Take the Girl Out of the Mountains But You Cannot take the Mountains Out of the Girl

Jennifer Kinsler

7 APPALACHIAN FAVORITES

Mountain folk are well known for their traditional foods, customs, common phrases, and superstitions. These are some of the things that set them apart from the outside world. Here are some of the ways we do/say things in the mountains along with some other favorites. We really don't care how the rest of the world says/does it.

FOODS:
Biscuits & Gravy, Grits
Sawmill gravy with Hog Jawl (sawmill = cornmeal)
Cornbread and Soup Beans
Hoe Cakes (cornbread fritters)
Taters (fried taters, tater cakes, smashed taters, tater salad)
Fried Bologna "Bloney"
Frog Legs (Many go frog gigging, even the children)
Rabbit Stew, Squirrel and Dumplins', Deer Meat
Fresh Garden Veggies
Apple Stack Cake, Rhubarb Pie
Fried Chicken, Chicken & Dumplins' (Especially a hit with preachers)
Fried Apples, Apple Butter, Molasses
Blackberry Dumplins', Strawberry Dumplins'
Poke Sallet (Polk Salad – type of cooked greens that grew wild)

DRINKS: Sweet Tea, coffee

Common Mountain Words:

A letter (a) added at the beginning of words: a-goin, a-runnin, a-watchin, a-workin, etc.

Many words are drawn out into two syllables (hee-yull = hill)

All words with an –ire sound are pronounced –ar (fire/far, tire/tar)

A long o sound at the end of words becomes –er (holler, foller, fellar)

Word	**Translation**
Y'uns/Ya'll	You Guys/You All
Naw	Disagree
Yender/Yander	Over yonder/over there
Hep'yee or hope yee	Help You
Mater	Tomato
Tater	Potato
Gaum	A mess
Thang/Sang/Fangers	Thing/Sing/Fingers
Skeered	Scared or afraid
Ary/Nary	Any or None
Warsh	Wash
Ort	Ought
Woe-mern	Woman
Stob	Stick
Thoe	Throw
Tote	To carry
Rern/Rernt	Ruined
Poke	Bag
Dope	Soda Pop
Ta-marr	Tomorrow
Mush melon	Cantaloupe
Lag	Leg
Ag	Egg
Lack	Like
Sup	Sip

Mountain Phrases:

Phrase	Meaning
"That's a plum blank lie"	Not the truth
"Pecker Wood" or "Jasper"	Idiot (Someone not liked)
"Mucha Bliged"	Thank You
"Rat Fur Piece"	Far
"Hottern Hell"	Very Warm
"Coldern Hell"	Chilly or very cold
"Ov-air"	Pointing to an area
"Prar Meetin"	Church Service
"That barnt/burnt me up"	Made angry
"Right Smart"	Large amount
"Coons age"	Long time
"Folded Up"	Went out of Business
"A Spell"	A while
"Don't git above your raisin"	Don't be stuck up
"Gulley Warsher"	Heavy Rain
"Sweetenin"	Dessert
"Well ain't you pretty?"	You're being hateful/ugly
"Finer n' frog hair"	Things are going well
"Jerk em' up by the hair of the head"	Pulling hair in a fight
"Looks to me like"	A statement of agreement
"A cake of soap"	Bar of soap
"Egg-turner"	Spatula
"Sundy/Mundy"	Sunday/Monday
"You're just puttin' on"	Pretending
"Tickled to death"	Very Pleased
"Flatter n' a Flitter"	Skinny
"My ears are burnin"	Someone talking about me
"Put on ye clodhoppers"	Farmer's work shoes
"Spoiled Brat"	A petted child
"That's hogwash"	A bunch of nonsense
"No use fer nothin'"	Lazy
"Who's yer momma's people?"	Who are your grandparents
"Well, bless your heart"	Your dumb/Feel sympathy
"He's as poor as Job's turkey"	Having little to no money
"I don't care if it harelips granny"	Don't care who it offends
"A little bird told me"	Keep secret who said it

Jennifer Kinsler

Mountain Superstitions/Sayings:

You can get warts by handlin' toads.
You will have seven years of bad luck if you break a mirror.
A four leaf clover will bring you good luck if you can find one.
A cat can take away a baby's breath, causing it to die.
Don't get in any water while menstruating or it will kill you.
If a black cat runs across the road in front of your car, it's bad luck.
Wear shoes outside or you'll get worms.
It's pert ner (close to) dark outside so don't be out after dark or the haint's will get you. (Ghosts of the dead/haunts)
Step on a crack and you'll break your mother's back.
Death comes in threes. When one dies, at least two more will soon die.
It's bad luck to walk under a ladder.
It's bad luck to open an umbrella in the house.
It's bad luck if a woman comes by your house before anyone else on New Year's Day.
Eat hog jowl, black-eyed peas, and greens on New Year's Day for good luck, plenty of money for the new year, etc.
If someone sweeps under your feet, you'll never get married.
If you tell your nightmare before you eat breakfast, it will come true.
For every fog in August, there will be a snowfall the following winter.
Seeing wooly worms are a sign of a bad winter.
Only pick up a coin if it's on heads side up or you'll have bad luck.
If your nose is itching it means somebody is coming to visit.
Go by the phases of the moon signs to plant gardens, go fishin', etc.
Aint that a sight for sore eyes! (Pleased to see)
Let's run to town and pay the juice bill. (Electric bill)

If you carried water in a bucket, that's how much your baby would slobber. The elder women would make the new mothers carry a thimble full of water back from the spring when first getting water. New mothers can't get out of bed until the baby is nine days old. Placing an axe under the bed of the delivering mother is said to "cut" some of the labor pain.

Mountain Remedies/Cures:

If a baby had mouth thrush, one could take it to an old woman and have her blow in the baby's mouth. This is said to cure it.

If a baby was colicky, one could pass it through a horse collar. This was supposed to cure the colic. It had to be done by two people.

Catnip tea will cure colic. It can be found growing wild. It also helps adults sleep when boiled and made into a tea.

Whiskey mixed with rock candy will cure the common cold.

Stating a certain bible verse will stop a bleeding wound instantly.

Witch Hazel as well as Solstice Salve is good for chest congestion. Once you apply to your chest, place a couple of blankets on you and lie in bed for a bit. You can also apply solstice to the feet and put socks on before going to bed.

Fresh tobacco spit is good for a bee sting. A cut of chewing tobacco also helps.

Creek mint is good for fever and is said to also be an antibiotic. It usually grows near creeks/springs and has a strong minty smell.

Pond's cold cream is good for the skin. It helps reduce wrinkles.

Vinegar is good for sunburn. It takes away the sting of the burn.

Karo Syrup will help with constipation.

Ginseng root is good for a number of ailments. Many mountain folk dig it regularly. It also helps provide an extra income for many families.

A swig of moonshine will cure a ton of ailments.

Jennifer Kinsler

8 HARD TIMES IN THE MOUNTAINS

Life wasn't always easy in the mountains. Into these hills and up the winding mountain roads was and is a place where children and families face unthinkable conditions. People who aren't accustomed to mountain life often take for granted just how fortunate they really are. Mountain folk have always been appreciative though, and they take pride in their land and heritage. Some mountain folk would rather die than ask for help while others have no other choice but to ask for help.

One such hard time fell upon my dad and his siblings back in the 1960-70's. They had just moved into the green house and didn't have any food to eat. Aunt Diana recalls being about four years old. Grandma Ethel was still living in Church Hill. Mammaw Betty had not told anyone they didn't have food but I am sure she prayed and asked the Lord to provide. She was a good person who took her children to church. She wasn't perfect, as no one is, but she was committed to do the Lord's will and seek His help. One day, a neighbor, Jenny Livesay, stopped by their house with some fresh garden vegetables. Jenny told Mammaw Betty that the Lord impressed her to gather up some food from the garden and bring it to them. Mammaw Betty told Jenny she hadn't been to the store and they didn't have anything to eat. The Lord always provides when we put our trust in him. Grandma Ethel once told me as young girl that "no home was complete without the Bible in it". She was affirming her faith to me when she said this. I never forgot it.

Grandma had a certain story she told everyone...everywhere she went. She told folks she "died twenty-one times". The look on the faces of those folks as she told this was priceless! Actually, the doctors had told her that her heart stopped beating at least twenty-one times while she was on the operating table. She was a living, breathing miracle! She had a pacemaker placed in her chest near her heart to help her heart beat at a normal rate. Back then, we had to be careful she wasn't around a microwave when in use because it might interfere with the electric signaling of the pacemaker. This was concluded to be a myth later on, however. We would have to ask her to go outside or into another room whenever we used a microwave. She did not have a microwave at her trailer but many places she visited did, including her granddaughter, Trish. She had to wear a special bracelet that could alert others she had a pacemaker in the unlikely event she became unconscious.

Grandma outlived her husband and both children. I cannot even begin to imagine the toll this took on her health. Death is cruel yet a part of life that we must all face eventually. My Papaw Paul Lucas, Dad's father, died in 1994 and this was so hard for all of us. He had cancer so we expected his death but that did not make it any easier to live with. Within six months, Uncle Harold died from a heart attack. Uncle Harold was saved at the funeral of my Papaw Paul. Harold, like his father, served in the military. From the age of 18, Harold served nearly three years before returning home and starting his family. I noticed grandma really changed after she lost her son. The cheerfulness in her face went to a sense of hopelessness for what seemed like an eternity. I am sure it was not the life she had imagined for herself or her children. Most mothers expect to die before their children do. Gilberta Maness, my Aunt Diana's mother-in-law, once told me there was no pain like losing a child. She stated she had given up her parents and others but nothing compared to the loss of a child. Grandma Ethel actually grieved herself to the point she nearly stopped eating. She only drank Ensure for nourishment for the longest time. Within two years, we lost her.

Losing a grandmother is to lose a most valuable family member. Especially when my grandmother had many times filled the shoes of a mother for me throughout my life. I was numb. My heart never felt so much pain. What a legend she was. What a great loss for our family. What an emptiness we all felt. No one really thinks about life without someone who means the most to them. She was my biggest supporter, my encourager, my secure place. I was only twenty-one years old at the time of her death. We were told we could come across to the Hawkins County Memorial Hospital to view her body before it was released to the coroner. I will never forget walking into that emergency room. Her body lying lifeless on a gurney. She looked like she was only asleep. I felt as if any moment she would just wake up and talk to us. Her skin was still lukewarm. This was my moment to say goodbye. So many memories flooded my soul at that moment. The only thing I knew was that I was full of hurt and still here to carry on what she taught me. As an old saying goes, "She taught me how to live but not how to live without her." Time has a way of easing the pain while the memories are there to provide comfort for all the years ahead.

    I learned so many things from knowing my Grandma Ethel. She was wise. Wise about life and death as she had experienced both. Her life spanned almost the whole of the 20th century. She had lived through the Great Depression, Recession, severe droughts and near famines. She lived during the time there was very little technology and when it began to boom to make life a bit easier. She had a huge impact on my life. We shared so many memories. Her time on earth was filled with family, friends, love, and some very interesting experiences. Because of my strong spiritual belief in Jesus Christ, I was able to cope with her loss and am now able to share her with a world who did not know her like I did. I know it wasn't goodbye that day in the ER but only "farewell, until I see you again."

    Life continued after we lost Grandma Ethel. However, just a few years later, around 2002, Cousin Rob was involved in a horrible accident. Several calls and searches were made but no one knew where Rob was. He had been missing almost an entire September day. The weather had just began to turn cold the night he went missing. Everyone was praying and continued to search but we all feared the worst. Someone thought they had last seen him on his four wheeler (ATV). Hugh Kyle Kinsler had been on Grandma's land putting corn out for deer in preparation for hunting later on. Hugh heard a dog barking so he moved closer to investigate what was going on. It was Rob's dog. It was at that time Hugh noticed someone trapped under a four wheeler. He went to call for help. The family was notified Rob had been found far back in the hills so the Rescue Squad was on its way. By the time I got there, the ambulance was backed up into the Jay Holler, had Rob loaded into the back, and were doing vitals on him before taking him on to the hospital. As I stood there that day, it was as if the Lord himself prompted me to get in that ambulance and have prayer with Rob. I hesitated for a minute not knowing if they would allow me to do so while also knowing how quickly he needed to be taken to the hospital. I then opened the back door and entered. I told the workers I needed to have prayer with Rob. They stopped what they were doing until I had finished praying. We later found out Rob had been paralyzed from the waist down. He had hit a tree stump with his four wheeler and it flipped into a tree and overturned with him underneath it. The impact crushed his spine instantly and he lie there all night long with that four wheeler on top of his body while not being able to move. The motor continued to run until it finally ran out of gas. We thought the four wheeler was probably what kept him from being frostbitten on such a cold night. How could this be? Surely, he would not be paralyzed the rest of his life. We visited him often throughout his time in the hospital, therapy, and home. He remained paralyzed for the next twelve years while only regaining some of his body movements. He had to use a wheelchair which caused infections often.

His kidneys and other organs were so stressed by the condition that he stayed in and out of hospitals and the nursing home during the latter part of his life.

    Despite his circumstances, Rob remained humorous. I visited him at the home of his sister Trish not long after the accident. I just felt so sorry for him and he sensed it. He said "Jenn, why are you standing there looking so sad?" He assured me there was nothing to be sad about. His positive attitude from his accident remained unchanged. He had accepted what happened to him. I didn't get to visit as often as I would have liked but when I did, he was always so glad to see me. I was working at an elementary school in 2014 when I had a strong urge to go visit him. I had heard his condition had worsened. I requested a Tuesday off so I traveled to Church Hill where Rob was staying. I spent that entire day with him. I had taken my family history binder to show him all the research I had done. By this time, he couldn't hear well, so I had to write everything I said on a dry erase board and wait for his response. We talked about old times. We laughed and nearly cried. He went through every page of my family history binder, one by one. He took time to reflect and tell me about some of the family he remembered or heard Grandma Ethel speak about. He was so excited to know I had put all this together. He asked me why I didn't write a book. I had never really thought about writing a book about our family. I did make copies of my binder as I told him I would and sent it for him to keep. That was the first and only time he looked through our family history binder. I made it a point that day to find out if he had been saved or not. He told me he had accepted Christ at Livesay's Chapel Church when he was fifteen years old. The hospice chaplain stopped by before I left so the chaplain made sure of this as well. The chaplain, Rob, and myself all had prayer together that day before I left. We were told a few days later that his condition had worsened. When Dad, Diana, Dougie and I went to visit the same week on a Saturday, he was in a hospital bed and could not speak. All the family was there. He made a few head nods to dad and pointed upward and that was about all he could do. We visited for a while with the family and left later that evening. We were informed he died only a couple of days later. I don't think it had even been a week since I sat there talking and laughing with him about the old days. Death is the same for all of us, whether we live in the mountains or in a fine mansion. We all have to experience death at some point. It is never easy to give up family to death. It just seems so cruel. When things happen in life, family is an anchor during all those rough waters. This is one of the things I learned from Grandma Ethel, who loved all of her family very much. The family unit is God's greatest masterpiece.

You Can Take the Girl Out of the Mountains But You Cannot take the Mountains Out of the Girl

Grandma eating fried chicken.
The 8 track player with tracks on top are to the right.
Clothes washed were often hung on top of the curtain rod to dry.

This photo was taken of Grandma Ethel the day we were going to her son Harold's funeral. It was taken at her Granddaughter Patricia's house.

Jennifer Kinsler

9 MOUNTAIN GIRL

I quickly learned to pick up and continue with life. My Grandmother Ethel had been a stable caregiver and created a desire in me for new experiences to add to the knowledge I already had. I married, raised two children, graduated with a Master's degree in Elementary Education, but ended up working with a ministry that serves two counties. One county we serve is where I currently live and the other one is in the mountains where I grew up. My mountains.

However, the mountain environment is somewhat different today. Families don't take the time to spend together as they once did. Everyone seems to be on a fast-paced schedule. The busyness of life often keeps many of us apart. Morals have declined dramatically in the last twenty years. Drug abuse is more rampant than it has ever been. A few living in the mountains feel as if they must move away to succeed in life. Many others are stuck with the little resources they have so they just try to make ends meet. There are few jobs available that pay well enough for a family to support themselves, even with a college education. One thing remains. The same mountains with all its challenges are still there. Opportunity comes in finding how to give back to the community by looking for ways to improve the plight of the people as well as yourself. Change, determination, and a drive to succeed only comes from within each person. All are given the same chance at life although certain barriers may hinder individual progress. Growing up in poverty with lack of resources didn't stand in my way of going on to succeed at something. I had a baby so I had to drop out of high school during the start of my sophomore year to take care of her. I had made the honor roll my freshmen year of high school but with a baby came a huge responsibility that prevented me from graduating. I was determined to take care of my baby on my own without help from anyone. I enrolled in homebound to finish out my sophomore year. Once my baby was older, we moved across the mountain to live with my Dad and step-mom until we could get our own place. Dad had remarried and moved to Hawkins County. Shannon's wages were not enough for us to afford our own home at the time. I worked several dead end jobs until I decided to sign up for GED classes in Rogersville. By this time, Shannon had a better job with more pay so we found our own place to rent for a few years. Mrs. Joy Debord was my GED teacher and she encouraged me to succeed. She was originally from Hancock County herself. I passed my GED test and a few years later enrolled in college. My daughter, Ashley, started Kindergarten so I wanted to continue my education. I earned my first Bachelor's degree and landed an interim position teaching in an elementary school in Hawkins County. I had signed up to be a substitute teacher prior to this so I would have more experience in a classroom setting. After completing several more interims, I went back to receive my Master's in Elementary Education thinking I would surely get hired since I had built up so much experience. With Shannon's job promotion, we had purchased our first home in June 2000. I worked in the public school system completing interims for at least seven years (2008-2015) and my last full year I worked as the Reading Interventionist for a local elementary school. I taught Kindergarten, First, and Third grades during these years while working with all grades K-5 as Interventionist. I worked in both Hawkins and Hancock County school systems. I was given high recommendations by several principals/teachers from both counties. Yet, with the political nature of a small community as well as repeated budget issues, I was never hired full time. I applied with several outside counties and interviewed several times but still saw no hope of a full time position. Lack of jobs are still prominent in the mountains. I decided to move on and look for something else when I joined with a local Lions Club. As chance would have it, our Lions Club wanted to paint the downstairs door of the local ministry in preparation for their anniversary celebration meeting. This is where I learned of an available position and soon accepted Director of Missions/Housing after a considerable amount of prayer and discussing it with my husband. This had to be where God had directed my steps. There was no doubt about it after I found out I could get my personal student loan debt set up on a public service loan forgiveness program. After my first summer with the ministry, the Director of Christmas for the Children retired so the ministry board made the decision to combine both positions into one and appointed me over the programs. This was very enjoyable but extremely challenging at times. Some work days lasted up to twelve hours and this exhausted me to no end. Plus, I wasn't very knowledgeable in construction work but I managed to oversee more than seventy home repairs with few issues. When not overseeing construction during the summer or the Christmas program from October-December, I worked with the ministry thrift store assisting with food pantry counseling, day to day operations within the store and finally took over managing the book/media section of the store. This was probably my favorite thing to do as I love reading books. I was appointed to take on the two entirely different programs and it just wasn't working out with no other staff persons to assist me. It was often difficult searching for grants and funding for the overwhelming amount of construction jobs that needed to be done. Ministry is very rewarding but often burn out comes within the first five years and this is where I found myself. After the second year had passed, I realized I needed to slow down and spend more time with my husband and our personal ministry. Shannon is an evangelist (traveling minister) so we had hoped to devote more time to this cause. He pastored a church for less than a year and filled in for a short time at the church we had attended for many years. He is currently filling in at Fox Branch Church in Kyles Ford until they find a pastor. We drive across the mountain every Sunday and this is the church just up the road from where my Grandmother Ethel lived. The church where my 3rd and 4th Great Grandmothers (Ida & Harriett) and their families attended during the early 1900's. It is also the church where my husband attended as a young boy and committed his life to Christ at the age of nine. I gave up the Director of Missions/Housing position but remained in the Christmas for the Children program. I also help out part time in other areas of the ministry as needed while still being able to assist the new director with mission teams on occasion. I enjoy this work very much. The program provides Christmas for children of families that would otherwise not be able to afford it. I screen applicants and verify income, proof of address, proof of eligible children and obtain children's clothing sizes as well as requested gift items. I then distribute the names and information to our local area churches who host a Christmas party during the month of December. Any remaining names not taken on by local churches are delegated to mission groups who travel to our area to host the parties. It gets very hectic during this season and I still work close to twelve hour days but only during the first three weeks in December. Our own children are grown and have moved out so working with the Christmas program only four months out of the year gives me some much needed free time. During this free time, I began writing this book. I wanted to have something to pass down to my children and future generations to preserve the memories I had. I have no idea what God has in store next, but I am anxious to see.

    As the old home places in Kyles Ford have succumbed to nature, the memories are still very much a part of me. As time continues, there will remain little evidence that life ever happened as it did in this little mountain section I call home-other than the stories I have written here. One day, I too, shall succumb to the nature of death and cease no more on this side of life. For now, the long abandoned mountain homes sit silent, lonely, yet beautiful to the one who knows its past and many secrets. Many are the never-revealed secrets kept by the mountain folk that eventually pass away with the passing of the life that carried them deep within. There were things I never knew, stories I never heard, and experiences I'll never have again as the years of my youth have fled.

This mountain girl has survived despite the many challenges. I have no desire to be wealthy or have the best that money can buy. We manage to have what we need and we are thankful for every bit of it. My mountains were always about family. Good people, hard work, a sense of pride about living in the mountains, a strong will to survive, and a place to call home. No matter how far away I roam, I always come back to the memories of my mountains.

You can take the girl out of the mountains, but you cannot take the mountains out of the girl.

Our family photo 2016

Ashley, Jennifer, Shannon, & Rebecca

Jennifer Kinsler

10 FAMILY PHOTOS

Singletary & Ida (Fletcher) Johnson in later years

Family Heirloom- 2-300 year old cape from the Bunch Family

Jennifer Kinsler

Harriet (Pridemore) Fletcher and her Granddaughter Ethel Johnson Owens. The house in this photo was destroyed by a cyclone in 1933

The "green house" in 2013   Grandma's trailer 2013

A "Bow Tie" quilt made by Ethel or possibly Betty that was given to me by Uncle Goob

You Can Take the Girl Out of the Mountains But You Cannot take the Mountains Out of the C

Back row: Papaw Paul Lucas & Randall Lucas (Dad)
Sitting: Uncle Eugene (Goob) Lucas & Diana Lucas Maness

ABOUT THE AUTHOR

Jennifer Kinsler was born and raised in the poverty stricken mountains of East Tennessee. She is a wife, mother of two daughters, and a ministry leader with a background in education. Jennifer continues to live and work in the Appalachian mountains.

Sources

Grohse, William Paul, papers (Microfilm) CD

Vardy Community Historical Society Sneedville TN

Hancock County Historical Society Sneedville Tennessee

Websites:

City-Data.com, http://www.city-data.com/city/Sneedville-Tennessee.html

Magazines:

Discover Hancock County Volumes I- II.

Made in the
USA
Columbia, SC